Academic Writing Skills

Student's Book 2

Peter Chin   Samuel Reid

Sean Wray   Yoko Yamazaki

CAMBRIDGE
UNIVERSITY PRESS

University Printing House, Cambridge CB2 8BS, United Kingdom

One Liberty Plaza, 20th Floor, New York, NY 10006, USA

477 Williamstown Road, Port Melbourne, VIC 3207, Australia

314–321, 3rd Floor, Plot 3, Splendor Forum, Jasola District Centre, New Delhi – 110025, India

103 Penang Road, #05-06/07, Visioncrest Commercial, Singapore 238467

Cambridge University Press is part of the University of Cambridge.

It furthers the University's mission by disseminating knowledge in the pursuit of education, learning and research at the highest international levels of excellence.

www.cambridge.org

This is the revised and expanded edition of *Academic Writing Skills and Strategies II*, ISBN 978-4-903049-15-1 first published in Japan by Waseda University International Co., Ltd. in 2007

© Cambridge University Press 2012

First published 2012

20 19 18 17 16 15 14 13

Printed in Malaysia by Vivar Printing

ISBN 978-1-107-62109-1 paperback Student's Book 2
ISBN 978-1-107-68236-8 paperback Teacher's Manual 2

Cambridge University Press has no responsibility for the persistence or accuracy of URLs for external or third-party internet websites referred to in this publication, and does not guarantee that any content on such websites is, or will remain, accurate or appropriate.

References and information relating to people, bodies corporate, places, e-mail addresses and website (with the exception of the Cambridge University Press website) in this publication may be fictitious or have been fictionalised, are for illustrative purpose only, are not intended to be factual and should not relied upon as factual.

Contributors: Adam Gyenes, Stephen Hurling, Dean Poland, Thatcher Spero
Editor: Sean Wray

Cover photo: ©iStockphoto.com/dkgilbey

Academic Writing Skills has been developed by the Research and Development team at Waseda University International Co., Ltd., Tokyo.

Contents

Introduction

Academic Writing Skills 2 reinforces key structures presented in *Academic Writing Skills 1* while introducing new essay elements, presenting more complex skills, and covering three distinct academic essay types.

There are four units in the textbook:

- Unit 1: Writing an Expository Essay
- Unit 2: Research and Citation
- Unit 3: Writing an Argumentative Essay
- Unit 4: Writing a Compare and Contrast Essay

Each unit presents explanations, examples, exercises, and model essays to help you attain university-level academic writing skills in research-based argumentative and compare and contrast essays. In particular, you will learn to:

- include a motive for an essay.
- create an indirect thesis statement.
- develop and include effective counter-arguments.
- develop and include logical rebuttals to counter-arguments.

Academic Writing Skills 2 also focuses on integrating outside sources into essays using citation – an essential skill in academic writing. The information and exercises presented will help you learn how to:

- identify shared language and common knowledge.
- quote, paraphrase, and summarize information from outside sources.
- add authority to outside sources, and integrate them effectively using reporting verbs.

To maximize the use of this book, you should:

- read the information in each unit thoroughly.
- take notes in the page margins with ideas and explanations from your teacher, classmates, or your own thoughts.
- complete all the exercises.

Dedicated study of *Academic Writing Skills 2* will prepare you with the necessary skills and strategies to successfully write a range of common academic essays.

UNIT 1

Writing an Expository Essay

Essay structure and the introductory paragraph

Essay structure

An essay is a piece of writing made up of a number of paragraphs. Each paragraph has a specific role in an essay. In a five-paragraph essay, the first paragraph is an introduction; the second, third, and fourth paragraphs form the body of the essay; and the fifth paragraph is a conclusion (see diagram on page 4). This book will focus exclusively on the five-paragraph essay. Although essays may vary in length, the five-paragraph essay structure can be adapted for longer or shorter essays.

1. Introductory paragraph

The first paragraph of an essay should introduce the reader to the essay topic. It should create interest in the essay, outline the writer's main ideas, and suggest how these ideas will be presented within the body of the essay. The introduction consists of three main elements: a **hook**, **building sentences**, and a **thesis statement**.

1. **Hook**

    The first sentence (or sentences) of an essay should catch the reader's attention. It introduces the topic of the essay in an interesting way.

2. **Building sentences**

    After the hook, the following sentences should provide background information to give readers some context about the topic. They should "build" towards the thesis statement.

3. **Thesis statement**

    The thesis statement comes at the end of the introduction. It is the most important sentence in the entire essay because it presents the essay topic and the writer's position on that topic. It also indicates the main ideas that will be discussed in the body paragraphs.

2. Body paragraphs

The body of an essay consists of three paragraphs. **Each body paragraph explains in detail one of the main ideas expressed in the thesis statement.** There are three parts to a body paragraph: a **topic sentence**, **supporting sentences**, and a **concluding sentence**.

1. **Topic sentence**

    The first sentence of a body paragraph expresses the topic of the paragraph and provides a controlling idea about the topic. All information in the paragraph supports the controlling idea.

2. **Supporting sentences**

    Supporting sentences explain and develop the topic sentence. They present logical thoughts, evidence, and explanations in support of the controlling idea.

3. **Concluding sentence**

    The paragraph may end with a concluding thought on the paragraph topic. It may also show a transition to the next paragraph.

3. Concluding paragraph

The concluding paragraph ends the essay by reviewing the main ideas from each body paragraph and leaving the reader with a final thought. The conclusion consists of three elements: a **restated thesis**, a **summary of main ideas**, and a **final thought**.

1. **Restated thesis**

    At the start of the conclusion, the thesis is restated in words different from those in the introduction.

2. **Summary of main ideas**

    The main ideas from each of the body paragraphs are summarized as a reminder to the reader.

3. **Final thought**

    The writer ends the essay by presenting a final thought on the topic – for example, by stating an opinion, a solution, or a prediction. The final thought should leave a strong impression and encourage the reader to think further about the topic.

Five-paragraph essay structure

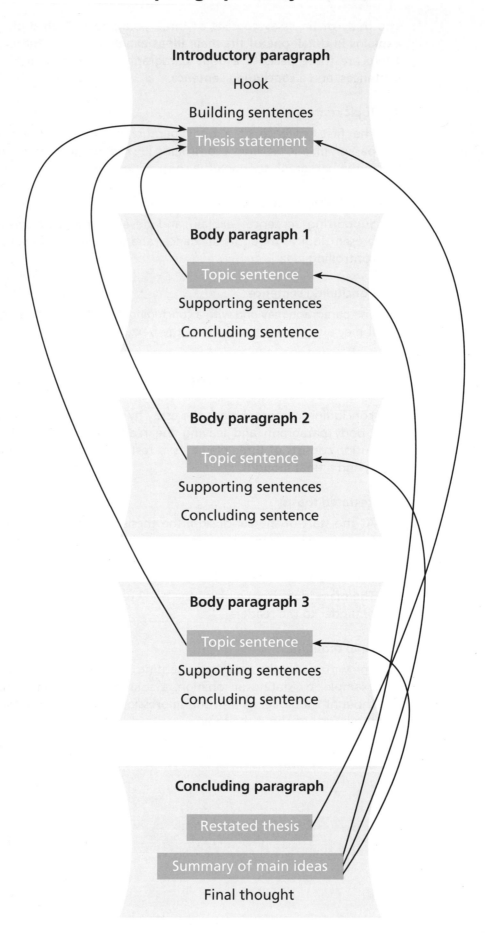

Introductory paragraph

Hook

Building sentences

Thesis statement

Body paragraph 1

Topic sentence

Supporting sentences

Concluding sentence

Body paragraph 2

Topic sentence

Supporting sentences

Concluding sentence

Body paragraph 3

Topic sentence

Supporting sentences

Concluding sentence

Concluding paragraph

Restated thesis

Summary of main ideas

Final thought

Exercise 1

The model essay below answers the following essay question:

Explain how an alternate form of energy is being used successfully in the world today.

Identify these elements in the following model essay.

1. Introduction, body, and conclusion.

2. The three main parts of the introduction.

3. The three main parts of each body paragraph.

4. The three main parts of the conclusion.

"I'd put my money on the sun and solar energy. What a source of power! I hope we don't have to wait until oil and coal run out before we tackle that." With this statement, Thomas Edison, the inventor of the light bulb, recognized the capacity of the sun as a virtually limitless source of energy in 1931. However, although a time when oil and coal have been completely used up could be getting closer, the full potential of solar power is yet to be harnessed by mankind. Televisions, refrigerators, air conditioners, and all the other appliances common in the developed world require vast amounts of electricity, meaning that the world's most powerful countries still very much depend on fossil fuels. In Sub-Saharan Africa, Southeast Asia, and parts of South America, however, solar power is already changing the lives of people who have until now lived without a steady electricity supply. As low-cost solar panels become available, they are being used most effectively in some of the world's poorest countries, which also happen to be some of the sunniest. Solar power is improving people's lives in developing countries by providing efficient light safely, linking them to the global mobile community and increasing their independence.

Low-cost, solar-powered lamps provide a dependable and safe source of light to people in rural communities who often have no connection to a national electricity grid. People either had to do without electricity, or were limited to using unreliable, low-intensity light from candles or kerosene lamps at night. Now, a new solar-powered lamp, when charged for eight hours in the bright sun, can provide up to a hundred hours of continuous, stable light ("Solar"). As a result, families are now able to extend and enrich their days by pursuing hobbies or crafts, and socializing longer into the evening with a brighter, constant light. Furthermore, solar power is clean and safe. An Energy Resource Group article reports, "Health problems caused by toxic fumes from kerosene lamps are responsible for an estimated two million deaths annually" (Silver). In addition, both candles and kerosene are a fire hazard, especially in homes that tend to be predominantly made of wood. Solar-powered lighting removes these dangers from people's homes because they emit no fumes and have no open flame, so people benefit from cleaner air and a reduced worry of fire. Solar power, therefore, has not only changed people's lives, it has also made their lives safer.

As well as providing reliable and safe light, the power of these solar panels is also being used to help people in developing countries connect to global communication networks. The same solar panel that provides light at night can be used to charge and recharge a cellular phone, which brings a number of significant benefits. For example, *New York Times* writer Sharon LaFraniere found that in rural, often remote parts of Sub-Saharan Africa, cell phones allow people to communicate easily and immediately with neighboring villages, as well as provide access to banking networks and global information sources (C3). The same article also reported that in a study of rural communities in developing countries, shop owners, traders, farmers, and fishermen all claimed that access to a cell phone had a positive impact on their profits (LaFraniere C3). As a result, their communities benefited economically. By providing a link to the world beyond the old limits of their immediate community, solar power is giving people in developing nations the means to improve their livelihoods.

Last, as a consequence of the technological benefits brought by solar power, people in developing countries are able to live their lives with greater autonomy. Solar power allows a poor family to make considerable financial savings. A BBC news story explains that a solar-powered lamp is relatively expensive for most families in developing countries, but because it costs nothing to operate after the purchase, it is much cheaper than alternatives, like kerosene ("Solar"). With their savings, more families can invest money into developing or expanding their farms or small businesses, which leads to greater financial stability and independence. Furthermore, solar power provides an environment in which people can educate themselves. In the journal *Africa Renewal – United Nations Department of Public Information*, it was concluded that literacy rates and the number of people studying for trade certificates are increasing faster in towns and villages where solar-powered lamps are accessible (Madamombe 10). Therefore, by allowing both children and adults to study at home in the evenings, solar power provides an opportunity for many people in the poorest parts of the world to escape a life of dependency through better education.

In summary, solar power is making a significant difference to the lives of people in the developing world. By providing safe, clean, and efficient light, it is removing dangers from people's homes while brightening their evenings. In addition, the ability to charge a cell phone allows people to communicate with the world and grow their businesses. The increased time and money available give people the means to take control of their lives and build for the future. The evidence certainly shows that in parts of the world where there is abundant sunlight, harnessing solar energy can be a key to improving the lives of many people.

Section 2   The introductory paragraph

The introductory paragraph should inform the reader of the essay's:
* topic.
* purpose.
* main ideas to be presented in the body paragraphs.

An effective introductory paragraph also creates interest in the topic and provides the reader with a strong reason to continue reading. It consists of three elements:
* a hook.
* building sentences.
* a thesis statement.

1. Writing a thesis statement

The thesis statement is the most important sentence in the essay because it specifically states what the essay will be about. In other words, it states the purpose of the essay. Therefore, a thesis statement should include:
* the topic of the essay.
* the writer's position, opinion, or approach to the topic.
* the main ideas that will develop and support the writer's position.

Also note the following about the thesis statement:
* It appears at the end of the introductory paragraph and, in short essays, is usually one sentence long.
* The main ideas are listed in the same order as they appear in the essay, which gives the reader a clear preview of what the following paragraphs will be about.

Example of a thesis statement:

Solar power is improving people's lives in developing countries by providing efficient light safely, linking them to the global mobile community, and increasing their independence.

This thesis statement shows that:
* "solar power" is the topic of the essay.
* the writer's position on this topic is that it is "improving people's lives in developing countries."
* the three main ideas that support the writer's position are a) it is "providing efficient light safely," b) it is "linking them to the global mobile community," and c) it is "increasing their independence." Each main idea will be explained in detail in a separate body paragraph: a) in the first body paragraph, b) in the second, and c) in the third.

It is useful to think of the thesis statement as the writer's answer to an essay question. Compare the essay question and thesis statement for the essay on page 5. The thesis statement provides a basic answer to the question, and the remainder of the essay will support this answer in greater detail.

Question:

Explain how an alternate form of energy is being used successfully in the world today.

Thesis statement:

Solar power is improving people's lives in developing countries by providing efficient light safely, linking them to the global mobile community, and increasing their independence.

Exercise 2

Read the following thesis statements. Where possible, underline the topic of the essay; the writer's position, opinion, or approach; and the three main ideas. Decide (✓ or ✗) whether each thesis statement has these parts or not.

1. (_____) South Korean dramas are popular because of the traditional values in these shows, the focus on romantic love, and the kindness of the male characters.

2. (_____) This is because smartphones allow us to connect to the internet, provide a range of useful and entertaining applications, and combine the functions of several electronic devices.

3. (_____) The internet has caused interest in daily newspapers to fall and may cause some newspapers to close.

4. (_____) Popular music changed dramatically in the 1990s for a number of reasons.

5. (_____) Rather than simply formulaic superhero stories, contemporary American comics cover a wide range of interests and themes, such as history, social problems, and human relationships.

2. Writing a "hook"

The hook is the first sentence of the essay, so it should create interest in the topic of the essay and encourage the reader to continue reading.

Use one of the following strategies to "hook" the reader.
1. **An eye-catching statement** uses an interesting idea or an idea opposing the thesis to introduce the topic.
2. **A surprising statistic** uses a detail that is not widely known to introduce the topic.
3. **A quotation (by an expert on the topic)** is a powerfully worded statement that begins the essay in a knowledgeable and authoritative way.

4. **A general truth** introduces something about the topic which the reader can immediately agree with.

5. **A question** gets the reader's attention by forcing them to think directly about the topic.

Exercise 3

Match each of the preceding strategies to the examples below.

1. "I dream of the realization of the unity of Africa, whereby its leaders combine in their efforts to solve the problems of this continent," stated Nobel laureate Nelson Mandela.

2. How would life be different in a world without electricity?

3. About 70% of people in Sub-Saharan Africa have no regular access to electricity.

4. For most people in the developing world, electricity is much like air: they use as much as they like without ever wondering where it came from.

5. There are some who see the coming of night as the time to stop work and the time to start enjoying their lives.

Exercise 4

An effective hook is often based on the general topic or theme of the thesis. Which of the following hooks a–e would be appropriate to begin the following introductory paragraph? There may be more than one answer.

One growing trend worldwide against this way of life is the "slow life" movement, which seeks a return to a simpler, more balanced lifestyle based on the appreciation of food and eating traditions. The slow life movement has successfully led to more and more people eating healthier food, a preference for locally produced over imported food, and an increase in the demand for organic and naturally grown crops.

a. People now have many more lifestyle choices than before.

b. When people move to cities, do they forget their traditional values?

c. Modern life for many people means enduring crowded streets, noise, endless advertisements, work, and stress.

d. Many young people today consider themselves part of the "Me" generation.

e. Although advances in technology were designed to make modern life easier and more convenient, many people have come to realize that they are busier and busier.

3. Writing building sentences

Building sentences help to provide a background to the essay and introduce any ideas or information necessary for the reader to understand the thesis. For example, building sentences could:

- explain the history of the topic.
- provide some statistics on the topic.
- mention the current situation regarding the topic.
- mention attitudes or opinions towards the topic.

Building sentences connect the hook, which introduces the essay topic in a very general way, to the thesis, which is a specific answer to the essay question. They can be presented:

- from general information to more specific information.
- using information familiar to the reader to information new to the reader.
- chronologically (from older information to newer information).

Consider the following example of building sentences organized using familiar to new information.

familiar information

"I'd put my money on the sun and solar energy. What a source of power! I hope we don't have to wait until oil and coal run out before we tackle that." With this statement, Thomas Edison, the inventor of the light bulb, recognized the capacity of the sun as a virtually limitless source of energy in 1931. However, although a time when oil and coal have been completely used up could be getting closer, the full potential of solar power is yet to be harnessed by mankind. Televisions, refrigerators, air conditioners, and all the other appliances common in the developed world require vast amounts of electricity, meaning that the world's most powerful countries still very much depend on fossil fuels. In Sub-Saharan Africa, Southeast Asia, and parts of South America, however, solar power is already changing the lives of people who have until now lived without a steady electricity supply. As low-cost solar panels become available, they are being used most effectively in some of the world's poorest countries, which also happen to be some of the sunniest. Solar power is improving people's lives in developing countries by providing efficient light safely, linking them to the global mobile community, and increasing their independence.

new information

Exercise 5

Below are two introductions. For each, put the building sentences in the right order to connect the hook and thesis statement.

1. **Topic:** The popularity of yoga

   Hook: In Sanskrit, the word *yoga* basically means "to unite."

   (_____) Yoga classes are now found in cities and towns around the world, and they are filled with people ranging from top athletes, to senior citizens, to young children.

   (_____) They are drawn by the opportunity to escape the stress of modern life by refreshing their tired minds and bodies in the quiet company of others.

   (_____) Although this might seem like a group or team commitment, it is actually a liberating personal experience.

   Thesis: Yoga is gaining in popularity around the world because it is accessible to all, reduces stress, and increases strength and flexibility.

2. **Topic:** The influence of Korean culture

   Hook: South Korea has become the little country with the big culture in East Asia.

   (_____) The ongoing "wave" also reached China, Thailand, and other parts of Southeast Asia, where Korean pop culture, food, and fashion are trendy.

   (_____) Described as the "Korean Wave," Korean culture first spread to Japan in the 1990s through popular TV dramas and films.

   (_____) This success has made Korean entertainers household names, and has created a great deal of interest in Korea and its culture.

   Thesis: Although it has now passed, the Korean Wave succeeded in making the Korean entertainment industry an economic force, greatly increased tourism to Korea, and helped establish South Korea as a genuine influence in East Asia.

For each topic below, read the hook and the thesis statement, and note down in point form what information should be included in the building sentences.

1. **Topic:** The threat of nuclear weapons

   Hook: Former British Prime Minister Margaret Thatcher once said, "A world without nuclear weapons would be less stable and more dangerous for all of us."

   Building sentences:

   _____

   _____

   _____

   _____

   Thesis: Nuclear weapons remain a major threat in the world because of terrorism, continuing conflicts between nations, and radical dictators.

2. **Topic:** Students studying abroad

   Hook: Is studying abroad something every student should do while in university?

   Building sentences:

   _____

   _____

   _____

   _____

   Thesis: The number of students studying abroad has been increasing because of the specialized programs available, the high status of a foreign degree, and the desire for a new experience.

Part 2 | Body paragraphs, concluding paragraphs, and outlining

The body paragraph

In a five-paragraph essay, the body refers to the three paragraphs that follow the introduction. The body paragraphs provide evidence in support of the writer's position, with **each paragraph organized around one main idea from the thesis statement**. Every sentence in a body paragraph should provide details and examples that only support this one main idea.

A body paragraph should include:
* a topic sentence.
* supporting sentences.
* a concluding sentence.

1. Writing a topic sentence

The topic sentence is the first sentence of a body paragraph. It has two parts:
* the **topic**.
* a **controlling idea**.

The controlling idea is what the writer wants to say about the topic. It "controls" the content of the paragraph. In other words, all of the following sentences in the paragraph should support this controlling idea. For example:

Low-cost, solar-powered lamps provide a dependable and safe source of light to people in rural communities who often have no connection to a national electricity grid.

Here the **topic** is "low-cost, solar-powered lamps" and the **controlling idea** is that they "provide a dependable source of light to people in rural communities."

NOTE: In a topic sentence, **do not:**
* introduce the topic with personal language.
    * ✗ *I am writing about the recent popularity of hybrid cars.*
* directly declare what will happen in the paragraph.
    * ✗ *This paragraph will examine the recent popularity of hybrid cars.*

The sentences on page 13 are too casual for academic writing. Instead, simply make the topic the subject of your topic sentence:

Hybrid cars are becoming increasingly popular because they are now affordable for more people.

Exercise 1

Read the following topic sentences, and circle the topic and underline the controlling idea where possible. Decide (✓ or ✗) whether each topic sentence is complete or not.

1. (_____) One major source of revenue for Thailand is food.

2. (_____) The second reason is that young people can use their laptops or tablets while drinking coffee.

3. (_____) Ghost stories reveal the traditional differences in social status between men and women.

4. (_____) So why did Bolivar do this?

5. (_____) Another problem with wind power turbines is that they often kill birds and bats.

2. Organizing supporting sentences

After introducing the controlling idea in the topic sentence, the supporting sentences should help show **why the controlling idea is true**. To do this, organize your supporting sentences in the following pattern:

1 = State a reason
- What is a reason for the controlling idea?
- What argument supports the controlling idea?

2 = Provide evidence
- What is an example of the reason?
- How is the reason demonstrated?

3 = Provide an explanation
- What do 1 and 2 mean?
- Why are 1 and 2 important?

This pattern is called the "waltz" (a kind of music with three beats). Following the waltz pattern helps develop ideas logically and creates well-organized paragraphs.

The waltz pattern may be repeated two or three times within a paragraph if the writer wishes to further support the controlling idea. Following is an example of how the waltz pattern can be used.

Topic sentence	Smoking causes a number of problems in restaurants.
Supporting sentences	
1. Reason **1**	Firstly, smoking can damage the health of people who work in restaurants.
2. Evidence	According to government research, working for four hours in a restaurant that permits smoking is the same as smoking six cigarettes.
3. Explanation	This shows that people who work in such restaurants for many years are exposed to risks that they cannot control.
1. Reason **2**	In addition, smoke can reduce customers' enjoyment of visiting a restaurant.
2. Evidence	For example, if smoke gets into people's mouths, they are less sensitive to taste, and particles of smoke may overpower delicate foods.
3. Explanation	For many people, the chance to eat delicious food is a reason for going to a restaurant, but cigarette smoke often spoils that chance.
Concluding sentence	Therefore, a smoking ban in all restaurants would allow employees and customers to feel comfortable because their health and ability to enjoy the experience would be better protected.

Exercise 2

Each reason, evidence, or explanation can be more than one sentence. Read the sample body paragraph again and do the task following it.

Smoking causes a number of problems in restaurants. Firstly, smoking can damage the health of people who work in restaurants. According to government research, working for four hours in a restaurant that permits smoking is the same as smoking six cigarettes. This shows that people who work in such restaurants for many years are exposed to risks that they cannot control. In addition, smoke can reduce customers' enjoyment of visiting a restaurant. For example, if smoke gets into people's mouths, they are less sensitive to taste, and particles of smoke may overpower delicate foods. For many people, the chance to eat delicious food is a reason for going to a restaurant, but cigarette smoke often spoils that chance. Therefore, a smoking ban in all restaurants would allow employees and customers to feel comfortable because their health and ability to enjoy the experience would be better protected.

Decide if sentences a and b are reason, evidence, or explanation and add them to an appropriate location in the body paragraph.

a.   More evidence is a recent report in the *Journal of Medical Science* which found that workers in smoking environments were more likely to develop cancer.

b.   As well, cigarette smoke causes many people to feel nauseous.

3. Writing a concluding sentence

For paragraphs with multiple reasons supporting the topic sentence, a concluding sentence may be necessary in order to:

• summarize the reasons in the paragraph.

• show how the reasons prove the writer's position in the thesis.

Read the thesis and paragraph below taken from the model essay on page 5. The function of the concluding sentence is to support the thesis. It summarizes how solar power improves people's lives.

Thesis:

Solar power is improving people's lives in developing countries by providing efficient light safely, linking them to the global mobile community, and increasing their independence.

Body Paragraph 1:

Low-cost, solar-powered lamps provide a dependable and safe source of light to people in rural communities who often have no connection to a national electricity grid. People either had to do without electricity, or were limited to using unreliable, low-intensity light from candles or kerosene lamps at night. Now, a new solar-powered lamp, when charged for eight hours in the bright sun, can provide up to a hundred hours of continuous, stable light ("Solar"). As a result, families are now able to extend and enrich their days by pursuing hobbies or crafts, and socializing longer into the evening with a brighter, constant light. Furthermore, solar power is clean and safe. An Energy Resource Group article reports, "Health problems caused by toxic fumes from kerosene lamps are responsible for an estimated two million deaths annually" (Silver). In addition, both candles and kerosene are a fire hazard, especially in homes that tend to be predominantly made of wood. Solar-powered lighting removes these dangers from people's homes because they emit no fumes and have no open flame, so people benefit from cleaner air and a reduced worry of fire. **Solar power, therefore, has not only changed people's lives, it has also made their lives safer.**

Exercise 3

Read the paragraph below and match each sentence to one of the following functions:

T = topic sentence
1 = reason
2 = evidence
3 = explanation
C = concluding sentence

1. (_____) One benefit of religious schools compared to public schools is that children spend their time with others who share the same values and religious beliefs. (_____) In religious schools, children are more likely to make friendships when they are surrounded by people from a similar background. (_____) For instance, they share the same cultural values and so have a more natural understanding of each other. (_____) Such friendships occur naturally in religious schools while in public schools, students may be afraid to even talk about their religion because it is different. (_____) In addition, children from religious homes who are forced to attend public schools may be bullied because they wear religious clothing. (_____) According to *The Times* newspaper, Muslim students who wear headscarves because of their religion often suffer insults or bullying in public schools. (_____) This problem simply does not happen in Muslim schools where all students wear the same religious clothing. (_____) Therefore, although students in public schools may meet students with the same religious background, it seems more likely that they will receive greater support and understanding in religious schools.

2. (_____) Several differences may be seen between home schools and public schools with regard to academic results. (_____) In the public school system, everyone is expected to progress at the same rate. (_____) Students are grouped together with the result that lower students cannot stop to ask questions and smart students cannot go faster. (_____) Children educated at home, on the other hand, can progress at their own pace because they are studying alone or in very small groups. (_____) This means that smart students can move on to more challenging material when they are ready. (_____) According to Whitley, gifted students educated either at home or at schools sometimes graduate early (76). (_____) This flexibility in terms of pace also means that students educated at home often achieve better academic results. (_____) According to CNN, last year 9% of students educated at home achieved a grade A in English, while only 3% of public school students did the same. (_____) All of this suggests that students educated at home have a better chance of higher academic achievement than students educated in public school.

The function of the concluding paragraph is to **reinforce the ideas** in the essay. It restates these ideas in order to remind the reader of the essay's important points. The concluding paragraph often makes a final comment which encourages the reader to think more about the essay topic.

Therefore, an effective concluding paragraph consists of three parts:
1. a restatement of the thesis topic and position.
2. a summary of the main ideas.
3. the writer's final thought.

1. Restating the thesis

At the beginning of the concluding paragraph, the topic and position in the thesis should be restated to remind the reader of the writer's position. When restating these, however, the writer should not use the same words or expressions used in the introduction:

Thesis:

Solar power is improving people's lives in developing countries by providing efficient light safely, linking them to the global mobile community, and increasing their independence.

Restated thesis:

In summary, solar power is making a significant difference to the lives of people in the developing world.

Exercise 4

Restate the following thesis statements.

1. Youth culture around the world has been significantly influenced by American youth culture as is evidenced by the music they listen to, the clothes they wear, and by the hobbies and sports they pursue.

    _____

    _____

    _____

2. Recently, practicing yoga has gained considerable popularity among young women since it is beneficial for their health, it helps relax their minds, and it is gentler than playing sports.

    _____

    _____

    _____

3. Smartphones have become useful in daily life not only as communication devices but also for everyday tasks such as paying bills, reserving tickets, and accessing bank accounts.

_____

_____

_____

2. Summarizing the main points

After restating the topic and position of the thesis, the next step is **summarizing the main idea of each body paragraph**. This summary helps remind readers of the important points which help support the writer's position. In summarizing the main points, however, the writer should avoid using the same phrases and expressions used in the body paragraphs.

3. Writing a final thought

An essay ends with the writer's final thought on the essay topic. A final thought can be:

• an opinion or judgment.

• a solution or recommendation.

• a prediction or speculation.

When writing a final thought, make sure it is directly related to the essay topic. Do not include any new details or examples which are not presented in the body of your essay. Introducing new ideas at the end of an essay may make the reader lose focus on the points made in the essay.

Read the concluding paragraph as an example:

summarized
main points

opinion final
thought

In summary, solar power is making a significant difference to the lives of people in the developing world. **By providing safe, clean, and efficient light, it is removing dangers from people's homes while brightening their evenings. In addition, the ability to charge a cell phone allows people to communicate with the world and grow their businesses. The increased time and money available give people the means to take control of their lives and build for the future.** The evidence certainly shows that in parts of the world where sunlight is in abundance, harnessing solar energy can be a key to improving the lives of many people.

Below are three final thoughts from an essay on measures to protect the dolphin population. In the parentheses under each example, write the function.

1. These measures to protect dolphins need to form part of a wider movement to increase humanity's respect for animal life.

   (_____)

2. If these measures can be successfully carried out, it is likely that the dolphin population will remain stable for the foreseeable future.

   (_____)

3. It seems that such measures can be usefully applied in protecting other species of animals which are facing similar population problems as dolphins.

   (_____)

Choose the most appropriate ending for the following conclusions.

1. In conclusion, it can be seen that learning a musical instrument offers young children a variety of benefits. Repeated practice during music lessons means children have the chance to become successful at mastering a skill, which is an important boost for their confidence. Furthermore, music provides a suitable environment in which to develop children's natural creativity and productive skills. Finally, children can derive a great deal of emotional and intellectual stimulation from an increased appreciation of music.

   a. However, with the recent popularity of other forms of entertainment, it is not clear how many children will take music lessons in the future.

   b. Clearly, it is the responsibility of the government to provide additional funding in order to increase the access children have to music lessons in schools.

   c. All this suggests that parents should think seriously about providing their children with these opportunities when they are growing up.

2. To sum up, cosmetic surgery is becoming more acceptable to people for a variety of reasons. First, because of the images promoted in the media, people are now inclined to put more value on physical beauty. Second, techniques for cosmetic surgery have advanced and now enable people to change their appearance more successfully. Finally, the cost of cosmetic surgery has become lower than ever before.

   a. The popularity of cosmetic surgery is the result of too much influence from the fashion industry. People should realize that real beauty does not lie in a person's appearance but in their mind.

b. Recently, there are many TV programs and websites which introduce people who have had cosmetic surgery and who explain how much their surgery cost. For people interested in having cosmetic surgery, such information is very useful in helping them make up their minds. They can start life as a new person.

c. For these reasons, it is no wonder more people want to have cosmetic surgery to feel more "attractive." There are still many people who feel uncomfortable with the idea of cosmetic surgery, but the trend will continue as long as there are people who pursue perfection in physical appearance.

Section 3 — Outlining an essay

Before writing, it is essential to create an outline of the essay. An outline is a plan of **what points will be included** in the introduction and body paragraphs. With an outline, the writer is better able to stay focused on the topic when writing the essay.

Before outlining, read the essay question carefully. Once the question is understood, follow the format below when outlining an essay. A strong essay outline will include a **thesis statement** as well as **topic sentences** and **supporting points** for each of the three body paragraphs.

NOTE: It is not always possible to write a perfect thesis on the first attempt. When outlining, it may be necessary to continue to change the thesis as new ideas are considered.

OUTLINE

Topic: *Write the topic at the top of the page here.*

Thesis statement:
Write the complete thesis statement here.

Body paragraph 1
Write the complete topic sentence for body paragraph 1 here.
- *Write supporting detail 1 here.*
- *Write supporting detail 2 here.*

Body paragraph 2
Write the complete topic sentence for body paragraph 2 here.
- *Write supporting detail 1 here.*
- *Write supporting detail 2 here.*

Body paragraph 3
Write the complete topic sentence for body paragraph 3 here.
- *Write supporting detail 1 here.*
- *Write supporting detail 2 here.*

Complete the outline below for the essay on solar power on pages 5–6.

OUTLINE

Topic: _____

Thesis statement:

_____

_____

Body paragraph 1
Topic sentence:

_____

_____

Supporting points:

1. _____

2. _____

Body paragraph 2
Topic sentence:

_____

_____

Supporting points:

1. _____

2. _____

Body paragraph 3
Topic sentence:

_____

_____

Supporting points:

1. _____

2. _____

Part

3 | Improving your work

Section 1 **Revising and editing**

At each stage of the writing process, it is important to stop and think about what you have written. For example, after writing a first draft, the writer should read it closely and make any changes necessary for improvement. This process is called **revising** and **editing**. Sometimes these words are used interchangeably, but in this book the distinction is made as follows:

- **Revising** – making changes to the content and organization of the essay.
- **Editing** – making changes to the vocabulary, grammar, and form of the sentences.

Revising and editing are essential in academic writing because they give the writer a chance to look at their work in a more critical way. In colleges and universities, **peer editing**, in which students revise each other's work, is also a common and useful exercise. Learning to edit increases the writer's independence, and makes them more able to assess their own work objectively.

To compose a successful academic essay, the writer needs to repeat the process of drafting and revising/editing **as many times as is necessary**. In general, this process may need to be repeated at least twice for short essays, such as a five-paragraph essay, and more times for longer essays.

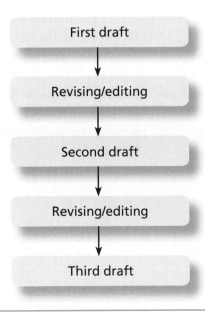

First draft

↓

Revising/editing

↓

Second draft

↓

Revising/editing

↓

Third draft

1. Writing for a reader

Every essay writer should be aware that "someone," a teacher or examiner, will read their essay. The reader of the essay will be both knowledgeable on the topic, and critical of your ideas. They will therefore expect that:

- the essay has been thoroughly researched.
- the essay shows a strong understanding of the topic.
- all ideas are presented clearly.
- all ideas are presented logically.
- the essay is effectively organized.
- the essay is objective in tone.

2. Academic tone

Using first- and second-person pronouns, such as *I, you, we,* makes the tone of writing subjective and informal, and so should be avoided in academic writing. In order to create the objective and formal tone necessary in academic essays, avoid using these words:

✗ *I believe we need to solve these problems.*

✓ *These problems need to be solved.*

✓ *It is necessary to solve these problems.*

✗ *There are many restaurants where you can eat endangered animals.*

✓ *There are many restaurants where endangered animals can be eaten.*

✗ *If our environment is not protected, our children will suffer the most.*

✓ *If the environment is not protected, children will suffer the most.*

✗ *We Cambodians do not usually shake hands, and instead make a little bow with hands clasped together.*

✓ *Most Cambodians do not usually shake hands, and instead make a little bow with hands clasped together.*

✓ *In Cambodia, people do not usually shake hands, and instead make a little bow with hands clasped together.*

Another way to make the tone of writing more objective and formal is to use less emotional words:

✗ *Learning to play a musical instrument is a wonderful experience for children.*

✓ *Learning to play a musical instrument is a beneficial experience for children.*

✓ *Learning to play a musical instrument is a positive experience for children.*

Section 2 Revising the content and organization

Many writers believe that all they need to do after writing the first draft is to correct grammatical mistakes. While correcting such errors is necessary, it is essential to **check the content and organization** of the essay first. If the organization is unclear or the content is presented illogically, then the essay will not be successful in its aims. Although each essay may have a different focus or objective, there are several common points to keep in mind when revising.

Checklist

The whole essay

1. Is the essay an appropriate length?

2. Does the essay avoid subjective language? Is the tone of writing objective?

3. Does all the information in the essay support the writer's position?

Introductory paragraph

4. Is there a "hook"? Does the hook make the reader want to continue reading?

5. Do the building sentences lead logically to the thesis statement?

6. Does the thesis statement include the topic, the writer's position on the topic, and the main ideas of each body paragraph?

Body paragraphs

7. Does the topic sentence show the topic and controlling idea of the paragraph?

8. Is all the information in the paragraph relevant to the controlling idea of the topic sentence?

9. Is the "waltz" used to organize and develop the paragraph's main idea?

Concluding paragraph

10. Is the thesis restated using different words?

11. Is there a summary of each main idea from the body paragraphs?

12. Is there a final thought? Does the essay feel completed by this?

13. Are new ideas avoided in the paragraph?

Using the checklist on page 25, revise the following draft.

The internet

Everybody uses the internet. Recently it has become common for people, not only in developed, but also developing countries to have it. It is no longer seen as something that is only used by people who are interested in computers, but it has become a part of modern life. The internet is having a significant impact of the internet on people's lives.

Firstly, it has allowed people to access information very easily. In the past, people could only learn about current events from newspapers that were sold where they lived, or by watching the news that was shown on their televisions. The internet has changed this. Now people are able to be much more informed about world events. As well, people are able to learn about topics that they are interested in much more easily. For example free online encyclopedias make it possible to get information on almost any subject. In addition students can easily find relevant resources, such as academic articles, for their studies. Consequently, they are able to write better essays. Therefore, I think that it is clear that the internet makes people more informed about the world around them.

Secondly, the internet has changed business. For example online retailers, such as Amazon, stock a wide range of goods. Rather than customers having to visit shops in order to buy the products that they want, it is now possible for them to view and buy a large range of goods from the comfort of their homes. This is a great thing as it means that people in rural areas, who in the past did not have access to a wide variety of products, can now enjoy shopping just like people who live in big cities. It is also good for the environment as it reduces how much people have to travel to do their shopping. Clearly if fewer people need to go into a city to do their shopping, then less pollution will be produced.

Finally, it is now possible to communicate with people more easily. In the past, living far apart from friends and family made it difficult and expensive to keep in contact, but the internet provides people with a number of cheap and easy ways to keep in touch. For example, people can use email to send letters and photos to people who are on the other side of the world. It is also possible for them use video conferencing applications to see and talk to people irrespective of the distance between them. As a result, people no longer feel that moving to a different city, country, or even continent will lead to less communication with their friends and families. This is another major impact of the internet on people's lives.

In conclusion, the internet has had a significant impact on people's lives. It has changed the way people get information, go shopping, and communicate. However it is important to note that there are many other ways in which the internet has affected people's lives, such as giving them the ability to download music and movies, play online games, and find new friends.

Section 3   Editing grammatical errors

After revising the content and organization of an essay, edit grammar. Accuracy in the following grammatical points is important for the clear presentation of ideas:
1. Capitalization in essay titles
2. Punctuation
3. Sentences and words

1. Capitalization in essay titles

Only the main words in a title should be capitalized. Do not capitalize articles (*a*, *an*, *the*), coordinating conjunctions (*and*, *but*, *or*, etc.), or prepositions (*of*, *to*, *for*, etc.) unless they are the first word in the title:

The Relationship between the Ancient and Modern Olympics

2. Punctuation

The comma

- Use a comma between independent clauses connected with a coordinating conjunction (*for*, *and*, *nor*, *but*, *or*, *yet*, *so*):

  *Many people wish to move out to the countryside for a slower pace of life, **but** few of them actually make up their minds to realize this dream.*

  Exception: The comma is not needed when the two independent clauses are short and the meaning cannot be misunderstood:

  Some people move to the countryside and they are happy about their choice.

- Use a comma to separate three or more items which are listed in a sentence:

  *Many high school students spend their time after school at shopping malls, fast food restaurants, **and** cafés.*

  *Young people often like to chat **and** text in cafés.* (two items – no comma)

- Use a comma when two or more adjectives are used to modify a noun:

  *Visiting Korea from China for a few days is an **easy, inexpensive** way to experience foreign culture.*

- Use a comma after an introductory phrase using a transitional expression:

  ***Before the appearance of Seattle-style cafés**, people rarely ordered coffee to take out.*

  ***First**, poverty is not a problem only in poor countries.*

- Use a comma to separate a non-restrictive relative clause and an appositive from the rest of the sentence:

  *Facebook, **which is a social networking service on the internet**, has become extremely popular among young people.*

  *Facebook, **a social networking service on the internet**, has become extremely popular among young people.*

Punctuation in relative clauses

- A relative clause is a clause which modifies the noun before or after it.

- A relative clause is called a **restrictive relative clause** when the information it carries is essential in the sentence:

  *Many people **who feel stress in their daily** life practice yoga to relax.*

  In the above example, the basic meaning of the sentence would change without the relative clause *(Many people practice yoga to relax)*.

- A relative clause is called a **non-restrictive relative clause** when the information it carries is **not** essential in the sentence. A non-restrictive clause in a sentence is put between commas:

  *Facebook, **which is a social networking service on the internet**, has become extremely popular among young people.*

  In the above example, the basic meaning of the sentence would not change without the relative clause *(Facebook has become extremely popular among young people)*.

- An **appositive** is a shortened form of a non-restrictive relative clause:

  *Facebook, **a social networking service on the internet**, has been extremely popular among young people.*

The colon

- Use a colon to introduce a list:

  When a person's family member passes away, it is said that they go through the stages of grief: denial, anger, bargaining, depression, and acceptance.

- Use a colon between independent clauses if the second clause adds a summary or explanation to the first clause:

  Creators of cell phones are modern day Alexander Graham Bells: they have dramatically changed how people communicate.

The semicolon

- Use a semicolon between two closely related independent clauses forming one sentence (see Appendix page 128):

  It became increasingly difficult for young people without solid experience to get a full-time job; many began to look for part-time work instead.

- Use a semicolon with a transitional expression to form a sentence with two independent clauses:

  *It became increasingly difficult for young people without solid experience to get a full-time job; **therefore**, many began to look for part-time work instead.*

Exercise 2

The following passage has mistakes in capitalization and punctuation. Identify and correct them.

> modern youth trends
>
> In the last three decades people's lifestyles have changed dramatically. Today it seems that more and more people are pursuing individual happiness, rather than collective satisfaction and this trend is more apparent among young people. Now many people who have graduated from school choose part-time employment and do not attend University. Researchers and Scientists do not know why? However one theory states that young people today feel unmotivated, because parents work longer away from home and they could not give the guidance children need.

3. Sentences and words

The writer should be aware of several problem areas concerning sentences and words:

- **Sentence fragments**

  Sentence fragments are incomplete sentences:

  ✗ *Because it is useful.*

  ✓ *Because it is useful, many people study English.*

- **Run-on sentences**

  In a run-on sentence, two or more independent clauses are included without any proper connectors:

  ✗ *People are attracted to new things, cell phone companies often upgrade existing models.*

  ✓ *People are attracted to new things, **so** cell phone companies often upgrade existing models.*

- **Parallel structure**

  In parallel structure, use the same word pattern to indicate that two or more ideas are equally important:

  ✗ *Some people like to shop at Gucci, and they like to shop at Saks, and shop at Tiffany.*

  ✓ *Some people like to shop at Gucci, Saks, and Tiffany.*

- **Subject–verb agreement**

  Verb form needs to agree with the subject:

  ✗ *Cafe latte and cafe mocha are popular item at Seattle-style cafés.*

  ✓ *Cafe latte and cafe mocha are popular item**s** at Seattle-style cafés.*

  ✗ *Once a month, he go to the museum to see new exhibitions*

  ✓ *Once a month, he **goes** to the museum to see new exhibitions.*

- **Verb tense**

  Verb form needs to agree with the tense of the sentence:

  ✗ *The first Europeans who come to New York buy Manhattan Island from the Native Americans for only $24.*

  ✓ *The first Europeans who **came** to New York **bought** Manhattan Island from the Native Americans for only $24.*

- **Word form**

  Use the correct word form depending on its function in the sentence:

  ✗ *In this global world, people can enjoy diversity cultures.* (noun + noun)

  ✓ *In this global world, people can enjoy **diverse cultures**.* (adjective + noun)

Exercise 3

The following passage has mistakes in sentences and words. Identify and correct them.

Many people like YouTube. Because it has many funny videos of people just like themselves. YouTube has become very popular people laugh the most when they see something strange about a situation who is very familiar to them. So when people see a cat swinging from curtains and a woman in a beautiful dress falling into a wedding cake they understand the situation. And they laugh since they these events are real but not a script from a comedian which is also funny but for another reason not really related to everyday life.

UNIT 2

Research and Citation

Part 1 Introduction to research and citation

Section 1 Finding sources for academic essays

Before writing an academic essay, students are required to **research** the essay topic. This research increases the writer's general knowledge of the topic and helps them form ideas to include in the essay. It also provides the writer with specific information and examples to support these ideas.

The following **sources** are often useful when researching an essay:
- books
- periodicals (journals, magazines, etc.).
- indexes
- databases
- reports

Before using any of these sources, it is important to check how **appropriate** they are by using the following criteria:

Authority
- What do you know about the author of the source?
- Are they established as an expert in their field?

Purpose
- Why was the source written?
- Is the author trying to persuade or simply inform the reader?
- Is the author writing formally, casually, or emotionally?

Intended audience
- Who is the target audience? (Some sources are prepared for a very specific audience, e.g., young children, and may not be appropriate for an academic essay.)

Relevance
- Was the source published recently?
- Is information in the source relevant to the essay topic?

When researching, be sure to keep a record of any sources that you wish to use in your essay. For each source, try to note as much of the following information as possible:

- author, title, and/or organization.
- publishing details (place/name/date).
- (for online sources) website address (URL) and date accessed.

You will need to list this information later when writing your essay (see "Creating a list of Works Cited" on page 51).

Exercise 1

Work with a partner. Answer the questions on page 32 of this textbook. Try to establish the book's authority, purpose, intended audience, and relevance.

Section 2   Plagiarism

Plagiarism is when ideas, words, or work from an outside source are **falsely presented as the essay writer's own**. In academic essays, it is expected that the essay writer will use information from outside sources. However, it is their responsibility to state where this information has come from.

Be careful of plagiarism when using:

- another person's ideas (e.g., opinions or theories).
- another person's exact words (written or spoken).
- information that is not widely known (e.g., facts, dates, statistics).

Plagiarism is regarded as a serious academic offense, and essays can be heavily penalized because of it. To avoid plagiarism, it is necessary to use both:

- quotation, paraphrasing, and/or summarizing and
- citation (see Unit 2, Part 2).

Section 3   Using outside sources in academic essays

There are three ways to present information from outside sources in an academic essay:

1. **Quotation**: using the exact words from another text and placing them inside quotation marks (" ").
2. **Paraphrasing**: putting information from another text into your own words.
3. **Summarizing**: making a summary of information from another text.

The essay writer must decide which of these three ways is the most effective each time they use outside information in their essay.

The following paragraph, taken from the model essay in Unit 1 on page 5, shows one example each of paraphrasing and quotation.

Low-cost, solar-powered lamps provide a dependable and safe source of light to people in rural communities who often have no connection to a national electricity grid. People either had to do without electricity, or were limited to using unreliable, low-intensity light from candles or kerosene lamps at night. Now, a new solar-powered lamp, when charged for eight hours in the bright sun, can provide up to a hundred hours of continuous, stable light ("Solar"). As a result, families are now able to extend and enrich their days by pursuing hobbies or crafts, and socializing longer into the evening with a brighter, constant light. Furthermore, solar power is clean and safe. An Energy Resource Group article reports, "Health problems caused by toxic fumes from kerosene lamps are responsible for an estimated two million deaths annually" (Silver). In addition, both candles and kerosene are a fire hazard, especially in homes that tend to be predominantly made of wood. Solar-powered lighting removes these dangers from people's homes because they emit no fumes and have no open flame, so people benefit from cleaner air and a reduced worry of fire. Solar power, therefore, has not only changed people's lives, it has also made their lives safer.

1. Quotation

Quotation is when the **exact words** are taken from an outside source and placed in an essay. These words appear inside quotation marks in the essay, and cannot be changed from how they appear in the source.

Quoting is a simple way of presenting other people's ideas in an essay, but it should not be used too often. Too many quotes will limit the essay writer's own voice in their own essay. Quotes should only be used when:

- the author of the quote is a respected authority on the essay topic.
- the words in the quote are memorably or succinctly expressed and make a strong impression on the reader.

2. Paraphrasing

Paraphrasing is when information is taken from an outside source and expressed in an essay **using the essay writer's own words**. The paraphrase uses roughly the same number of words as in the original source.

Paraphrasing is used when the writer wishes to use all the information from a passage. It is suitable to paraphrase short pieces of information (generally three sentences or less in length.)

3. Summarizing

Summarizing is another way that information is taken from an outside source and expressed using the essay writer's own words. However, a summary uses **fewer words than the original**; many summaries will only be one or two sentences in length.

Summarizing is used when the writer wishes to use only the main ideas from a source. It is a suitable way to include information from longer sources (from four sentences to a whole book in length).

The process of deciding how to present your sources in an essay is shown below. The essay writer must decide which of these three ways (quotation, paraphrasing, or summarizing) is the most effective each time outside information is used in the essay.

a. The original text is impressive and you want to use it as it is.	**b.** The original text is **short** (up to three sentences) and you want to use **all the ideas**.	**c.** The original text is **long** (more than three sentences) and you want to use **only the most important ideas**.
↓	↓	↓
Quote the information.	**Paraphrase the information.**	**Summarize the information.**

Section 4	Shared language

An important step in the process of paraphrasing and summarizing is to identify any shared language. The term *shared language* refers to words or phrases in the original source that should **remain the same**, such as:

- Proper nouns
  President Mandela, the World Cup, New Zealand, the Red Cross
- Common nouns
  police, bed, zebra, helicopter
- Dates and figures
  July, 1977, 18%, 4,900
- Specialized language
  blood pressure, penalty kick, economic recession

These words or phrases do not belong to any one writer. They are understood and used with the same meaning by everyone. It is therefore unnecessary to change shared language in an essay. For example, writing "a four-legged animal, with black and white stripes, resembling a horse" instead of using the common noun *zebra* would be confusing and inefficient. Similarly, the number *4,900* need not be changed to "almost 5,000."

Read the following paragraph and underline any shared language.

One of the clearest examples of animal culture can be found in the behavior of a group of bottlenose dolphins in Shark Bay, Australia. The dolphins pick up sea sponges from the bottom of the sea and wear them on their noses for protection when looking for food. Of a total 130 dolphins living in the area, only one extended family group of around 20 displays this behavior. This suggests that the use of the sponges as a tool is being learned and passed on within the group.

Section 5   Writing a paraphrase

Use the following steps as a guide when writing a paraphrase.

Step 1   Read and understand the original source.

Step 2   Note down any shared language on another piece of paper.

Step 3   Note down the details of the original in point form on the same piece of paper as the shared language.

Step 4   Using only the notes of the shared language and details, try to rewrite the information in your own words.

Do	Do not
• ... change the vocabulary.	• ... change the meaning of the source.
• ... change the word forms.	• ... add new information.
• ... change the structure.	• ... change shared language.
• ... keep a similar number of words as the original.	• ... use more than three words in a row from the original.

Step 5   Check your paraphrase against the original source.
- Has the original meaning been kept?
- Has plagiarism been avoided by using your own words, phrases, and grammar?
- Are roughly the same number of words used in the paraphrase as in the original?

Step 6   Add the paraphrase to the essay with a sentence or sentences explaining the relevance of this information. Be sure to use the correct citation.

Exercise 3

Read the passage below and the three possible paraphrases. Based on the criteria from Step 4, which of the possible paraphrases is best? Give reasons to support your answer.

Original source:
"Ska is a musical style characterized by an upbeat tempo and offbeat rhythm that originated in the 1950s in Jamaica. Influenced by jazz and rhythm and blues heard on American radio stations from cities such as New Orleans, Jamaican musicians fused these with Caribbean musical styles to create ska."

a. In the 1950s, the Jamaican style of music known as "ska," with its up-tempo feel and accentuated offbeat rhythm, developed from a fusion of Caribbean music and jazz or rhythm and blues heard by musicians in Jamaica on the radio from New Orleans and other U.S. cities.

b. The musical style called ska originally came from Jamaica in the 1950s. Jamaican musicians were influenced by jazz and rhythm and blues which they first listened to on radio stations from American cities such as New Orleans. They combined this with traditional Caribbean music to create a new upbeat, rhythmical style of music.

c. Ska music was born in Jamaica during the 1950s. Local musicians copied music that they heard on American radio stations from New Orleans among other U.S. cities. They used offbeat rhythms and a fast tempo to create a new Caribbean musical style.

Exercise 4

Using the steps on page 36, paraphrase the following passages.

1. "A large wave of Caribbean immigrants began coming to the United Kingdom after World War II, filling gaps in the labor market and seeking a better life. However, many experienced racism and difficulties finding jobs and housing when they arrived. Eventually they were able to settle and form communities that have now integrated into British society."

_____

_____

_____

_____

2. "London's Notting Hill Carnival is held over two days in August every year. It is a celebration of Caribbean culture and arts in the Notting Hill area, where many Caribbean immigrants to London first settled. It has grown to become the world's second largest street festival, attracting over two million visitors annually."

_____

_____

_____

_____

3. "In the late 1970s, a new generation of musicians started to play ska in England. They crossed ska with rock and punk styles to create a harder, more aggressive sound. Many of these bands promoted racial unity with their multiracial lineups and songs that raised awareness of racial issues."

_____

_____

_____

_____

Section 6   Writing a summary

Use the following steps as a guide when writing a summary.

Step 1   Read the original source until it is fully understood.

Step 2   Note down the main ideas and any shared language.

Step 3   Using only the notes of the main ideas and shared language, rewrite the information using your own words:
- Do not use more than three words in a row from the original as this will be regarded as plagiarism.
- Do not change the meaning of any of the ideas from the original or try to add your own thoughts.

Step 4   Check your summary against the original source:
- Has the original meaning been kept?
- Has plagiarism been avoided by using your own words?
- Are far fewer words used in the summary than in the original? Is the summary one or two sentences in length?

Step 5   Add the summary to the essay, with a sentence explaining the relevance of this information. Be sure to use the correct citation.

Exercise 5   **Read the passage below and the three possible summaries. Based on the criteria from Step 4 above, which of the possible summaries is best? Give reasons to support your answer.**

Original source:

"In every corner of the globe, aboriginal and traditional cultures are slowly disappearing. From the 18th century onwards, the processes of industrialization and the settlement of new people has had a dramatic effect on aboriginal groups such as the Australian Aborigines, the Teleut people of Siberia and the Ainu of Japan. These traditional cultures have survived for hundreds, sometimes thousands of years and their languages, music and other customs display a rich and wide variety of human culture. Yet these cultures risk being lost forever, as the old ways gradually die out and are replaced by more modern, industrialized lifestyles."

a. Today the cultures of indigenous groups such as the Teleut in Siberia or the Ainu in Japan are under threat. For around the last 200 years, industrialization and migration have weakened the cultures and customs of these groups. As a consequence, the survival of many different lifestyles is uncertain and the world risks losing forever its valuable diversity.

b. The twin processes of industrialization and migration have led to the demise of traditional cultures around the world, with many languages and customs potentially vanishing forever.

c. Aboriginal cultures, such as those in Australia or Japan, are valuable because they represent a wealth of musical, linguistic, and ceremonial traditions.

Exercise 6

Using the steps on page 38, summarize the following passages.

1. "Although the term *indigenous people* is applied to a large variety of different groups in many different parts of the globe, indigenous people can be broadly defined as a group that historically belong to one area or country pre-dating its colonization by a new dominant group, and whose culture, language, and traditions are distinct and unique, having developed entirely separately from those of the new group."

_____

_____

_____

_____

_____

2. "There are thought to be around 5,000 indigenous groups in over 70 countries worldwide. In some cases, only very few members of these groups remain while in others there may be hundreds of thousands. There are many groups that have been completely wiped out because of war, disease, or government policies. In many countries, those that remain have been dispossessed of their land and valuable natural resources, creating a situation in which they struggle to maintain their livelihoods, which typically depend on access to farming, fishing, and hunting grounds."

_____

_____

_____

_____

_____

3. "Indigenous peoples frequently rank among the most impoverished of all ethnic groups within a nation. In the United States, Native American communities on reservations are some of the most disadvantaged groups. Lack of education and high unemployment rates have confounded their low socio-economic status and have caused a host of social problems, such as alcoholism, teenage pregnancy, high crime rates, and a range of health issues. The limited opportunities have led to many Native Americans leaving their reservations and traditions to assimilate into mainstream American society."

_____

_____

_____

_____

_____

2 | In-text citation and the Works Cited list

Introduction

When using outside information in an essay, it is essential to cite the sources used in the text of the essay as well as to provide a list of all the sources cited in the essay.

Citation means showing the origin of the outside source information. It has two parts:

- in-text citation.
- Works Cited list.

1. In-text citation

When quoting, paraphrasing, or summarizing outside information in an essay, the writer must indicate the source of that information in the text. This is needed so that:

- the reader can find the exact location of the information in the original source.
- the writer can avoid being accused of plagiarism.

In-text citation generally requires the author of the source and the page number in the source where the information was taken from. In-text citation can appear in an essay in several ways. One way can be like the following example:

*Literacy rates and the number of people studying for trade certificates are increasing faster in towns and villages where solar-powered lamps are accessible **(Madamombe 10).***

author's last name and page number

summarized information from source

2. Works Cited

A Works Cited page is an **alphabetically ordered list of all sources** cited in an essay. It is attached at the end of the essay as a separate page, and provides complete information on where each source can be found. The Works Cited list helps the reader to:

- see the extent and quality of research the writer has done for the essay.
- find the original sources easily and gain additional information if interested.

The Works Cited entry for the in-text citation on the previous page would be:

Madamombe, Itai. "Solar Power: Cheap Energy Source for Africa." *Africa Renewal – United Nations Department of Public Information* 20.3 (2006): 10. Print.

NOTE: There are many different styles of citation. This textbook uses the Modern Language Association (MLA) style.

Section 2	Citing sources in the essay text

It is sometimes difficult to decide whether information requires in-text citation or not. Citation is required when using:

- a quotation.
- a paraphrase.
- a summary.
- information that is not widely known (e.g., specific numbers, maps, graphs).

Citation is not required if:

- ideas, opinions, and interpretations are the essay writer's own.
- the information is common knowledge.

1. Common knowledge

Information is considered common knowledge if it is an established fact. If information from a source can easily be found in many sources and its accuracy is accepted by the majority of people, it is probably common knowledge.
Examples:

a. *Millions of people have been killed in wars.*

b. *It is estimated that 17,656,000 people died during World War I.*

c. *A molecule of water is composed of one oxygen and two hydrogen atoms.*

d. *Pure water (H_2O) naturally has no taste or odor, so when spring and mineral water drinks claim to be "more pure," they are generally indicating their water is free of pollutants and microbes.*

In the above examples, statements **a** and **c** do not require citation because the information is widely known and accepted. However, statements **b** and **d** require citation because the information can be doubted or not fully accepted as true.

NOTE: If in doubt as to whether information is common knowledge or not, it is always safer to cite the source.

Exercise 1   **Decide if the following information requires citation or not.**

1. The population of China is over one billion.

2. By 2040, India's population is predicted to reach 1.52 billion.

3. Research has shown that there are important differences between written and spoken English.

4. The capital city of Australia is Canberra.

5. Yuri Gagarin was the first man in space.

6. Sea levels are expected to be 1.4 meters higher in 2100 than they were in 1990.

2. Using in-text citation

Two key elements are generally required to create in-text citation:
- the author (either a person or organization).
- the page number in the source from where information was taken.

The author is the first piece of information from each entry on the Works Cited list. This is normally either the author's last name, or the organization's name.

There are **two basic patterns** which can be used to add in-text citations into essays.

Pattern 1

The author's name is included in the sentence, in the following order:

author's last name, or organization name + quote, paraphrase, or summary of source information + (page number).

Examples:

Eliot claims that culture, not genetics, explains why girls tend to prefer pink, and that boys tend to prefer blue (213).

According to UNICEF, women often remain undernourished, and when they marry and become pregnant at a young age, they are highly vulnerable to sickness and disease (32).

Reporting verbs

Although the phrase *according to* is frequently used to introduce the author and source information, reporting verbs can also be used with Pattern 1 to express the **author's position** on the information. Choose the reporting verb that best represents the author's position on the information.

Reporting verbs include, but are not limited to, the following:

argue	claim	note	show
state	suggest	believe	indicate
found	conclude	point out	assert

Examples:

*Estés **believes** that every woman is free to abandon whatever is holding her back in order to regain her true, instinctual wildness (17).*

The World Health Organization argues that improving health is an integral part of improving both economic prosperity and social justice (2).

Adding authority to a source

When citing an unknown person, group, or organization, it may be necessary to **establish their authority** to the reader by including a description of their position or background.

Example 1:

✗ *James Richardson claims that the popularity of the book is due to its focus on adult issues (B2).*

✓ *James Richardson, **literary critic for the London Herald**, claims that the popularity of the book is due to its focus on adult issues (B2).*

In example 1, the second sentence is better because it informs the reader that Richardson has expertise about his topic.

Example 2:

✗ *According to People for the Ethical Treatment of Animals (PETA), some animals are more intelligent than humans (3).*

✓ *According to People for the Ethical Treatment of Animals (PETA), **an outspoken animal rights organization**, some animals are more intelligent than humans (3).*

In example 2, the brief description of the organization in the second sentence helps the reader better understand their position on the topic.

Pattern 2

The source name is included in parentheses at the end of the sentence:

> quote, paraphrase, or summary of source information   +   (author's last name/ organization name + page number).

Examples:

*Culture, not genetics, explains why girls tend to prefer pink, and that boys tend to prefer blue **(Eliot 213)**.*

*Women often remain undernourished, and when they marry and become pregnant at a young age, they are highly vulnerable to sickness and disease **(UNICEF 32)**.*

Pattern 2 is more appropriate when:

- the writer thinks the origin of the source is not important enough for the reader's attention.
- the writer wishes to focus the reader's attention on the information more than the source.

Sources with no author

For sources that **do not have an author**, or when the author is **unknown**, the first piece of information in the Works Cited entry should be used to create the in-text citation. This piece of information is normally the name of an article. The following Works Cited entry has the title of the article as the first piece of information:

> "Enhancing Pan-Continental Aid Efficiency in the 21st Century." *Aid Initiative Foundation*. Global Recovery Initiative, Apr. 2008. Web. 10 June 2011. <http://www.imf.org/external/publicdomaindocuments/eng/doc.html>.

The titles of articles appear in quotation marks in essays and in Works Cited lists. To create in-text citation using Pattern 1, the entire title must be used.

Example:

> *In "Enhancing Pan-Continental Aid Efficiency in the 21st Century," it was found that "Ethiopia has addressed this issue by implementing price controls over a wide range of daily necessities, including both food and non-food items" (34).*

To create in-text citation with the title of an article using Pattern 2, use only the first or first few content words (i.e., not grammar words) of the title.

Example:

> *"Ethiopia has addressed this issue by implementing price controls over a wide range of daily necessities, including both food and non-food items" ("Enhancing" 34).*

Sources with no page number

In some cases, a page number cannot be included because the source **has no page numbers**, such as with online sources. In this situation, only the first piece of information from the Works Cited list entry is included in the sentence (Pattern 1) or in parentheses (Pattern 2).

Examples:

Bowerman *reported in a Food and Drug Administration study that pesticide residues are found in more than 25% of the food which was tested randomly.*

*A Food and Drug Administration study found that pesticide residues are found in more than 25% of the food which was tested randomly **(Bowerman)**.*

Secondhand information

Secondhand information is information in a source which is **taken from another source**. For example, sources such as articles or books often use quotes, statistics, facts, or data from other sources. There are certain ways in which secondhand information is cited.

When the original source uses a quote from another source, cite both the secondhand source and the original source. Use the phrase *qtd. in* in front of the original source in the in-text citation:

The rising cost of energy, especially oil, has been affecting people's lives in many ways. James Stuart, Assistant Bureau Manager at the Ministry of Energy said, "The price of oil in the first quarter of the year has increased by 20% from the same period of the last year. This is certainly a difficult time for us" **(qtd. in Moore 76)**.

Exercise 2

Below is the essay from Unit 1. Read it again and answer the questions following the essay about the sources and citation in the essay.

"I'd put my money on the sun and solar energy. What a source of power! I hope we don't have to wait until oil and coal run out before we tackle that." With this statement, Thomas Edison, the inventor of the light bulb, recognized the capacity of the sun as a virtually limitless source of energy in 1931. However, although a time when oil and coal have been completely used up could be getting closer, the full potential of solar power is yet to be harnessed by mankind. Televisions, refrigerators, air conditioners, and all the other appliances common in the developed world require vast amounts of electricity, meaning that the world's most powerful countries still very much depend on fossil fuels. In Sub-Saharan Africa, Southeast Asia, and parts of South America, however, solar power is already changing the lives of people who have until now lived without a steady electricity supply. As low-cost solar panels become available, they are being used most effectively in some of the world's poorest countries, which also happen to be some of the sunniest. Solar power is improving people's lives in developing countries by providing efficient light safely, linking them to the global mobile community, and increasing their independence.

Low-cost, solar-powered lamps provide a dependable and safe source of light to people in rural communities who often have no connection to a national electricity grid. People either had to do without electricity, or were limited to using unreliable, low-intensity light from candles or kerosene lamps at night. Now, a new solar-powered lamp, when charged for eight hours in the bright sun, can provide up to a hundred hours of continuous, stable light ("Solar"). As a result, families are now able to extend and enrich their days by pursuing hobbies or crafts, and socializing longer into the evening with a brighter, constant light. Furthermore, solar power is clean and safe. An Energy Resource Group article reports, "Health problems caused by toxic fumes from kerosene lamps are responsible for an estimated two million deaths annually" (Silver). In addition, both candles and kerosene are a fire hazard, especially in homes that tend to be predominantly made of wood. Solar-powered lighting removes these dangers from people's homes because they emit no fumes and have no open flame, so people benefit from cleaner air and a reduced worry of fire. Solar power, therefore, has not only changed people's lives, it has also made their lives safer.

As well as providing reliable and safe light, the power of these solar panels is also being used to help people in developing countries connect to global communication networks. The same solar panel that provides light at night can be used to charge and recharge a cellular phone, which brings a number of significant benefits. For example, *New York Times* writer Sharon LaFraniere found that in rural, often remote parts of Sub-Saharan Africa, cell phones allow people to communicate easily and immediately with neighboring villages, as well as provide access to banking networks and global information sources (C3). The same article also reported that in a study of rural communities in developing countries, shop owners, traders, farmers, and fishermen all claimed that access to a cell phone had a positive impact on their profits (LaFraniere C3). As a result, their communities benefited economically. By providing a link to the world beyond the old limits of their immediate community, solar power is giving people in developing nations the means to improve their livelihoods.

Last, as a consequence of the technological benefits brought by solar power, people in developing countries are able to live their lives with greater autonomy. Solar power allows a poor family to make considerable financial savings. A BBC news story explains that a solar-powered lamp is relatively expensive for most families in developing countries, but because it costs nothing to operate after the purchase, it is much cheaper than alternatives, like kerosene ("Solar"). With their savings, more families can invest money into developing or expanding their farms or small businesses, which leads to greater financial stability and independence. Furthermore, solar power provides an environment in which people can educate themselves. In the journal *Africa Renewal – United Nations Department of Public Information*, it was concluded that literacy rates and the number of people studying for trade certificates are increasing faster in towns and villages where solar-powered lamps are accessible (Madamombe 10). Therefore, by allowing both children and adults to study at home in the evenings, solar power provides an opportunity for many people in the poorest parts of the world to escape a life of depedency through better education.

In summary, solar power is making a significant difference to the lives of people in the developing world. By providing safe, clean, and efficient light, it is removing dangers from people's homes while brightening their evenings. In addition, the ability to charge a cell phone allows people to communicate with the world and grow their businesses. The increased time and money available give people the means to take control of their lives and build for the future. The evidence certainly shows that in parts of the world where there is abundant sunlight, harnessing solar energy can be a key to improving the lives of many people.

Works Cited

LaFraniere, Sharon. "Cellphones Catapult Rural Africa to 21st Century."
  The New York Times [New York] 25 Aug. 2005, International sec.: C3.
  Print.

Madamombe, Itai. "Solar Power: Cheap Energy Source for Africa." *Africa
  Renewal – United Nations Department of Public Information* 20.3
  (2006): 10. Print.

Silver, Kelly. "The Transition to Safe Energy: Solar Advantages." Web log
  post. *Investigating Green Alternatives*. Energy Resource Group. 11
  Apr. 2009. Web. 21 Mar. 2011. <http://blogs.iga.org/solar>.

"Solar Loans Light Up Rural India." *BBC News – Home*. 29 Apr.
  2007. Web. 17 Mar. 2011. <http://news.bbc.co.uk/2/hi/science/
  nature/6600213.stm>.

---

1. How many citations are used in the essay?

2. Underline the information in the essay that was taken from sources.

3. What words or phrases are used to introduce sources?

4. How are the sources in the Works Cited list organized?

5. Are all the sources on the Works Cited list used in the essay?

6. Which source has no author? How does it appear in the essay? Why does it appear this way?

7. Why is information such as the *"Energy Resource Group,"* the "New York Times," the "BBC," and the "United Nations" included in the essay text?

8. What information from the Works Cited list must always be used to create in-text citation? Give examples for each in-text citation to show this.

9. Which in-text citation patterns were used with each citation? Why might the writer have chosen to use Pattern 1 or Pattern 2 in these situations?

Below are the thesis statement and the first body paragraph of an essay. The body paragraph is missing supporting evidence. Select the most appropriate quote or paraphrase to provide supporting evidence, and integrate it into the paragraph using an appropriate citation pattern and style.

Thesis statement
The recent decline in the reading of books can be illustrated in a number of different ways; books are being bought but are not being read, other forms of written media are increasing, and other forms of entertainment are more popular.

Body paragraph 1
Although more books are being bought than ever before in history, these books are not being read. One reason is that many people buy books in order to find specific pieces of information that they need for their jobs and hobbies. This has led to a large number of specialized books being published. _____

_____

_____

_____. One consequence of this is that many books are used only as a reference and they are not read from cover to cover. Also, people buy books that they think they should read, but often do not find enough time to finish them. _____

_____

_____. Although people seem to have the intention of reading books, they clearly lack the motivation to actually sit down and spend time reading them. Furthermore, people collect books as status symbols to show their knowledge. _____

_____

_____. This shows that people are buying books, not for the pleasure of reading them, but rather because they feel that simply owning them has a positive effect. Clearly people are still motivated to buy books, but many do not have the desire to actually read them; this may partly be due to the other forms of entertainment that are available to them.

Evidence and source information

1. "Reading books has given way to the status of possessing books." (Quote by the literary critic Malcolm Riggs.)

Author:	Gowri Davinder
Article Title:	"Notes on Urban Reading Trends"
Internet Site Name:	*SydneyStandard.com*
Publication Date:	August 1, 1998
Page Number:	no page number

2. In 2004, 15% of books that were published in the U.K. were scientific or technical. (Paraphrase)

Author:	Unknown
Article Title:	"No End in Sight"
Journal Name:	*The UK Publishing Review*
Date of Publication:	January 2005
Page Number:	9

3. A large number of the self-help books that are bought are never read. (Paraphrase)

Author:	Joseph Hunter
Book Title:	*New Water from the Well*
City of Publication:	London
Publisher:	Hartford-Quinn
Year of Publication:	2005
Page Number:	67–68

Section 3   Creating a Works Cited list

In addition to in-text citation, the writer is required to provide a Works Cited list at the end of the essay. To create entries manually, follow the patterns below according to the type of source listed.

NOTE: Many software applications and online services are available that create Works Cited lists automatically.

1 A book

author's last name, first name. *book title*. city where published: publisher. year of publication.

Example:

Wilson, Edward O. *The Future of Life*. New York: Alfred A. Knopf. 2002.

2 A journal article

author's last name, first name. "article title." *journal name*, date of publication: pages.

Example:

Ott, Robert. "Everyday Exposure to Toxic Pollutants." *Scientific American* Feb. 1998: 41–43.

3 A newspaper article (electronically retrieved)

author's last name, first name. "article title." *newspaper name*, date of publication. date of access. <URL>.

Example:

Bascaramurty, Dakshana. "Parental Stress and Pollution May Raise Asthma Risk in Kids." *The Globe and Mail*, July 2009. Web. 03 June 2011. <http://www.theglobeandmail.com/life/health/parental-stress-and-pollution-may-raise-asthma-risk-kids/article1226312/>.

4 Information on a website

author's last name, first name. "title of the document." *name of the website*. date of publication. organization name. date of access. <URL>.

Example:

Marshall, Leon. "Stockpiled Pesticides Harming African People, Environment." *Nationalgeographic.com*. 4 Nov. 2005. National Geographic Society. Web. 21 Dec. 2006. <http://news. nationalgeographic.com/news/2005/11/1104_051104_africa_toxins. html>.

5 Information on a government website

government. agency name. *publication title*. date of publication. date of access. <URL>.

Example:

United States. Environmental Protection Agency. *Effects of Acid Rain: Human Health*. 5 Oct. 2006. Web. 20 Dec. 2006. <http://www.epa.gov/ airmarkets/acidrain/effects/health.html>.

6 Missing information for the Works Cited entry

If the source does not provide all the information needed for a Works Cited list entry, simply cite the information which is available. In the following example, the source does not provide the author's name, so the name is omitted from the Works Cited list entry.

Example:

"National Geographic Society At-a-glance." *Nationalgeographic.com*. 2006. National Geographic Society. Web. 20 Dec. 2006. <http://press. nationalgeographic.com/pressroom/index.jsp?pageID=factSheets_detail& siteID=1&cid=1052839802576>.

To create a Works Cited page follow these rules:

- Each source is single-spaced (not double-spaced).
- A line is left between each source.
- The second and following lines of each source are indented.
- If a web address (URL) does not fit on one line, it can be divided and continue on the next line.
- If a web address is underlined, remove the line. Add the word *Web* before the date accessed.
- Add the word *Print* for non-digital sources at the end of the entry.
- Add *PDF* for sources that are in portable document format at the end of the entry.
- Use the title Works Cited in the middle of the page at the top.

NOTE: Refer to official MLA resources for the most up-to-date style versions.

If the example entries on pages 43–46 were to appear together on a Works Cited page, they would look as follows:

Works Cited

Bowerman, Karen. "Tests Spark Pesticide Concerns." *BBC News - Health*. BBC, 20 Sept. 2000. Web. 10 June 2011. <http://news.bbc.co.uk/1/hi/health/933141.stm>.

Eliot, Lise. *Pink Brain, Blue Brain: How Small Differences Grow into Troublesome Gaps – and What We Can Do about It*. Boston: Houghton Mifflin Harcourt, 2009. Print.

Estés, Clarissa Pinkola. *Women Who Run with the Wolves: Myths and Stories of the Wild Woman Archetype*. New York: Ballantine, 1997. Print.

Moore, Darragh. *All the King's Oil*. San Francisco: Brickside & Bonner, 2009. Print.

People for the Ethical Treatment of Animals (PETA). "Animals Are Not as Intelligent or Advanced as Humans." *About PETA*. Peta.org. Web. 7 July 2011. <http://www.peta.org/about/faq/Animals-are-not-as-intelligent-or-advanced-as-humans.aspx>.

Richardson, James. "Where Do Echoes Go to Die?" *London Herald* [London] 3 May 2007, Arts sec.: B2. Print.

UNICEF. *The State of the World's Children 2011: Adolescence – An Age of Opportunity*. New York: UNICEF, Feb. 2011. PDF.

World Health Organization. "The World Health Report: Health Systems Financing: the Path to Universal Coverage." *The World Health Report*. World Health Organization, 2010. Web. 09 June 2011. <http://www.who.int/whr/2010/en/index.html>.

Exercise 4

Create a Works Cited list from the following sources.

Author name:	Beverly Daniel Tatum
Title:	Why Are All the Black Kids Sitting Together in the Cafeteria?
Information type:	Book
Publisher name:	Basic Books
Published location:	New York
Published date:	1997

Author name:	George Packer
Title:	Knowing the Enemy
Information type:	Magazine article
Magazine title:	The New Yorker
Publication date:	Dec. 18, 2006
Page numbers:	from pages 60 to 69

Author name:	Not available
Title:	World's Education Leaders: Support Teachers
Information type:	Webpage article
Webpage title:	AskAsia.org
Sponsor name for the webpage:	Asia Society
URL:	http://asiasociety.org/education-learning/ learning-world/worlds-education-leaders-support-teachers
Updated date:	2011
Accessed date:	April 12, 2011

Author name:	Nigeria
Title:	Quality Education Central to Our Agenda for National Transformation
Information type:	Article on a government website
Webpage title:	Nigeriafirst.org
Organization name:	Office of Public Communication
URL:	http://www.nigeriafirst.org/article_11089. shtml
Date published:	May 18, 2011
Accessed date:	June 19, 2011

Works Cited

UNIT 3

Writing an Argumentative Essay

1 Developing arguments

Section 1   An argumentative essay

In an argumentative essay, the writer **takes a position** on an issue and **presents an argument** to convince the reader that the position is acceptable. The writer's argument needs to include:

- **logically explained opinions**.
- **authoritative evidence** (e.g., facts, examples, statistics).
- **counter-arguments** (possible objections to the writer's argument).
- **rebuttals** (reasons why the counter-arguments are not correct or weaker).

Including the items above helps ensure the writer's argument is convincing and shows that the writer has considered the issue completely.

The pre-writing steps for an argumentative essay are:

1. Read the question and establish a basic **position to support**.
2. Research sources to find evidence and ideas to **support the position**.
3. Consider **counter-arguments** and prepare **rebuttals** to them.
4. Write a thesis statement and outline the essay.

Exercise 1   Read the following essay and answer the questions.

1. What is the topic of the essay?

2. What is the writer's argument (i.e., position on the topic)?

The Democratizing of Knowledge: in Defense of Wikipedia

As the internet gained popularity, many hoped it would develop as a decentralizing and democratizing force where people could share information and learn from each other. Wikipedia, a free online encyclopedia and the world's largest reference resource, embodies such ideals in allowing multiple users to write and revise content. This collaborative practice differs from the process of compiling conventional encyclopedias, which relies on scholars

---

and experts to contribute information. Wikipedia's underlying belief is that by having more participants contributing and editing information, each entry will have greater range, depth, and accuracy. Some, however, claim such thinking is naive and fundamentally flawed due to the belief that a reliance on amateur editors will lead to inaccurate and unreliable entries. Yet, Wikipedia does provide a useful starting point for research, offering a comprehensive overview of complex topics, a neutral editorial stance, and a dedicated commitment to quality.

Launched in 2001, Wikipedia has become a valuable resource of information in a relatively short amount of time. One reason for this quick growth and for its reliability is the collective participation of a vast range of contributors from around the world. The number of people who contribute or edit information on Wikipedia is in the hundreds of thousands (Soneff). Furthermore, these contributions have to be facts that are verifiable, and entries must be unbiased and based on secondary research. Researchers at Dartmouth College concluded that these large numbers and the rules for contribution indicate that Wikipedia users are accessing information which is constantly being updated and checked for errors, therefore ensuring the information is accurate, which is a feature not available with traditional encyclopedias. Wikipedia's value is also evident in the breadth of information available. Olivia Solon, news editor at Wired.co.uk states that Wikipedia carries over 3.5 million entries across a diverse variety of topics ranging from the technical to the trivial. Furthermore, Wikipedia features hyperlinks within entries to related topics/terms, providing users with direct access to additional sources which may lead to a deeper understanding of a topic. Moreover, Wikipedia is not exclusive to those who can read English: not only is it one of the most frequented websites in the world, but it is also a multilingual resource with 270 non-English Wikipedia sites ("User-generated"). The result is a website which is a useful "one-stop" resource for research across disciplines and languages. The success of Wikipedia, therefore, has democratized knowledge through its vast amount of accurate and up-to-date information, and through its belief that any responsible user or contributor can access and add knowledge for the benefit of all people.

Together with its vast scope, the principle that all Wikipedia entries should be comprehensive and balanced makes it an especially valuable research tool. Academic research involves grappling with complex issues, concepts, or events, which is precisely what Wikipedia does. For example, the term *globalization* is especially controversial. For many, globalization means exploitation and widespread injustice (Scheve and Slaughter 4); for others, globalization is a beneficial force (Wolf 36). This disparity means it is especially important for researchers to comprehensively understand why the term is so controversial. Wikipedia, with its large number of contributors representing a range of possible points of view, provides detailed descriptions, the variety of perspectives on the issue, and the reasons for the controversy. Wikipedia's policy also ensures that neutrality is maintained, which is crucial for academic research on issues which are fiercely contested. Globalization issues involve pro-globalization and anti-globalization arguments, but both sides are described comprehensively in the Wikipedia entry on the topic. Indeed, this is only possible because Wikipedia is a free, Web-based resource that presents the breadth and depth of meanings associated with complex, contentious terms in a balanced way. This accessibility to unbiased information helps ensure that research results are accurate because the user is able to analyze and carefully consider all sides of an issue.

Despite such benefits, Wikipedia continues to attract critics, who claim there are significant weaknesses with its philosophy of complete openness. One perceived weakness is with the contributors, many of whom are not scholars or experts on the topics to which they add or alter information. The worry is that Wikipedia, by having entries which anyone can edit, is not a dependable resource because it is filled with incorrect, biased information ("Wikipedia"). Nevertheless, Wikipedia does employ a dedicated team of volunteer administrators whose job it is to quickly remedy inaccurate information. Furthermore, controversial entries can be tagged to indicate when information is under dispute and to encourage users to investigate the dispute and provide more input. Professor of communications Jonathan Thornton maintains that "the service revolves around a set of procedures that are carefully designed to ensure accurate articles through sufficient self-policing and self-amending." A study by the journal *Nature* indeed showed that Wikipedia is nearly as accurate as *Britannica* (Giles 900). A further concern is over vandalism of entries with false, malicious information, often aiming to hurt the reputation of certain people or organizations. However, this matter is being addressed through various measures. For example, software is being developed to swiftly detect words not consistent with the content of particular entries ("Tool"). All of this demonstrates both the commitment and ability to achieve increasingly higher levels of quality in Wikipedia.

To conclude, Wikipedia, with its breadth, depth, and reliability, serves as an excellent starting point for researchers of virtually any topic. It features millions of entries across a wide range of topics which are updated constantly. Researchers can confidently turn to it for comprehensive and mostly unbiased information on even the most complex and controversial of topics. While some fear that having too many contributors will lead to inaccurate and even harmful content, measures to ensure that the quality of the entries is maintained have allowed Wikipedia to achieve a level of accuracy close to that of other, more conventional encyclopedias. Though not perfect, Wikipedia has demonstrated that the potential of the internet to decentralize sources of information and empower people can be achieved.

Works Cited

Dartmouth College. "Power of Altruism Confirmed in Wikipedia Contributions." *ScienceDaily*, 19 Oct. 2007. Web. 22 Jun. 2011. <http://www.sciencedaily.com/releases/2007/10/071017131854.htm>.

Giles, Jim. "Internet Encyclopaedias Go Head to Head." *Nature* 438.15 (2005): 900–01. Print.

Scheve, Kenneth F., and Matthew J. Slaughter. *Globalization and the Perceptions of American Workers*. Washington, DC: Institute for International Economics, 2001. Print.

Solon, Olivia. "The Battle to Make Wikipedia More Welcoming." *Future Technology News and Reviews*. Wired.co.uk, 11 Jan. 2010. Web. 22 June 2011. <http://www.wired.co.uk/news/archive/2011-01/10/making-wikipedia-more-welcoming?page=all>.

Soneff, Steven. "Wikipedia: What Percentage of Wikipedia Users Actively Contribute? How Many Contributors Does Wikipedia Have?" *Quora*. 2 Dec. 2010. Web. 22 June 2011. <http://www.quora.com/Wikipedia/What-percentage-of-Wikipedia-users-actively-contribute-How-many-contributors-does-Wikipedia- have>.

Thornton, Jonathan. "An Assessment of the Accuracy of Wikipedia Editorial Policy." *Communication Technology Ideas and Issues*. 15 Mar. 2011. Web. 23 June 2011. <http://communication.technology.ideas.and.issues/0-18_3-153.html>.

"Tool to Improve Wikipedia Accuracy Developed." *News & Articles in Science, Health, Environment & Technology*. Science Daily, 26 Sept. 2010. Web. 22 June 2011. <http://www.sciencedaily.com/releases/2010/09/100924212131.htm>.

"User-generated Content: Wikipleadia." The Economist – World News, Politics, Economics, Business & Finance. The Economist, 13 Jan. 2011. Web. 22 June 2011. <http://www.economist.com/node/17911276>.

"Wikipedia Faces the Facts over Inaccuracy – Times Online." *Technology – the Timesonline.co.uk*. Times Newspapers Ltd., 20 Sept. 2007. Web. 22 June 2011. <http://technology.timesonline.co.uk/tol/news/tech_and_web/the_web/article2490895.ece>.

Wolf, Martin. *Why Globalization Works*. New Haven, CT: Yale Nota Bene, 2005. Print.

In an argumentative essay, the writer needs to **include counter-arguments** (possible objections to the writer's argument) and **refute them** with stronger rebuttals (rejections of the counter-arguments). Doing this makes the writer's argument more persuasive to the reader, and strengthens the essay by showing that the writer has considered all sides of the issue.

Example:

Essay topic: Capital punishment

The writer's argument: Capital punishment should be abolished for humane reasons.

1. Writer's position

Capital punishment should be abolished.

2. Counter-argument

Capital punishment should not be abolished because criminals deserve to die and it deters serious crime.

3. Writer's rebuttal

Killing criminals is an outdated idea, and there is evidence which indicates that the death penalty has no effect on crime rates.

counter-argument

rebuttal

There is certainly a group of people who insist on continuing the practice of capital punishment. They seem to believe that when a death sentence is carried out, it demonstrates that justice can be served and acts as a deterrent to crime. However, the concept of "an eye for an eye" is an outdated belief in modern times, when human rights are emphasized and guaranteed. In addition, Lamperti revealed that in the United States, where some states have the death penalty, and others do not, there is no variation in homicide rates between these states (14). To sum up, such an outdated practice should be abolished as it is clear that it does not seem to make any difference in reducing the occurrence of crime.

Exercise 2

What are possible counter-arguments to the following arguments?

1. Argument:

   All universities should send their students abroad for a year so that they can learn the language and culture of a different country.

   A possible counter-argument:

   _____

   _____

   _____

   _____

2. Argument:

   When university graduates apply for jobs, companies should request them to submit their academic grades so that students will become more serious about their work in university.

   A possible counter-argument:

   _____

   _____

   _____

   _____

3. Argument:

   Since the purpose of universities is to provide an environment to maximize a person's potential, students with high athletic ability should be admitted to university regardless of their academic ability.

   A possible counter-argument:

   _____

   _____

   _____

   _____

Along with counter-arguments, the writer must present effective rebuttals to convince the reader that the writer's own argument is stronger. This is done by:

- replying directly to each counter-argument.

- showing why each counter-argument is incorrect or insignificant.

Example:

✗ *One perceived weakness is with the contributors, many of whom are not scholars or experts on the topics to which they add or alter information. The worry is that Wikipedia, by having entries which anyone can edit, is not a dependable resource because it is filled with incorrect, biased information ("Wikipedia"). Nevertheless, the number of new entries added to Wikipedia annually continues to increase along with the number of new users.*

✓ *One perceived weakness is with the contributors, many of whom are not scholars or experts on the topics to which they add or alter information. The worry is that Wikipedia, by having entries which anyone can edit, is not a dependable resource because it is filled with incorrect, biased information ("Wikipedia"). Nevertheless, Wikipedia does employ a dedicated team of volunteer administrators whose job it is to quickly remedy inaccurate information. Furthermore, controversial entries can be tagged to indicate when information is under dispute and to encourage users to investigate the dispute and provide more input.*

The first example is an ineffective rebuttal because it does not address the counter-argument directly. The writer's rebuttal is off-topic because it focuses on the increasing amount of information and users of Wikipedia rather than the fact that there is incorrect and biased information on Wikipedia, which is the focus of the counter-argument.

The second example is an effective rebuttal because it directly addresses the counter-argument and explains specific measures which Wikipedia takes to ensure the correctness of the information on their website. As a result, the writer's argument that Wikipedia can be a reliable source of information is also strengthened.

Exercise 3

Choose (✓) the most effective rebuttal for each counter-argument. Discuss why the remaining rebuttals are ineffective.

1. Counter-argument:

   It has been argued that private lessons allow students greater freedom to talk about their personal interests.

   Rebuttal:

   (_____) Nevertheless, students can talk with more people in a group class. In terms of learning a language, this gives students more opportunities to talk, to share information, and to become more independent. Consequently, students in group classes will probably develop at a quicker rate than in private classes.

   (_____) Nevertheless, in terms of learning a language, it is not always best to spend too long discussing personal interests. In private classes, there is always a danger that lessons can become nothing more than casual conversations about familiar topics, thus limiting a student's chances to develop.

2. Counter-argument:

   Some people claim that students in private classes learn better because their teachers have a better understanding of their strengths and weaknesses.

   Rebuttal:

   (_____) While it is true that teachers in private lessons may have a very good understanding of their students' abilities, the same is also true for teachers of students in group classes. If students in a group class are at the same level, then they will share the same problems and, guided by the teacher, can help each other improve. In a private class, however, having a teacher continually point out a student's mistakes can be demotivating.

   (_____) While it is true that teachers in private lessons will have a very good understanding of their students' abilities, this does not necessarily mean that private lessons are more effective. Students in private lessons are under pressure for long periods of time and so often use more basic grammar and vocabulary (Hatton 14). In contrast, students in group classes are more likely to develop strong listening skills.

Exercise 4

Present rebuttals to the counter-arguments in Exercise 2 (page 61).

An argumentative essay follows the basic five-paragraph essay structure. However, there are two organizational frameworks that can be used to include counter-arguments in the essay.

Framework A		Framework B
Introduction	Paragraph 1	**Introduction**
Body paragraph 1 - Develop argument 1	Paragraph 2	**Body paragraph 1** - Develop argument 1 - Counter-argument 1 - Rebuttal 1
Body paragraph 2 - Develop argument 2	Paragraph 3	**Body paragraph 2** - Develop argument 2 - Counter-argument 2 - Rebuttal 2
Body paragraph 3 - Counter-arguments - Rebuttals	Paragraph 4	**Body paragraph 3** - Develop argument 3 - Counter-argument 3 - Rebuttal 3
Conclusion	Paragraph 5	**Conclusion**

In **Framework A**, the first two body paragraphs present the writer's argument. The counter-argument and the rebuttals do not appear until the third body paragraph.

In **Framework B**, the writer's argument is presented and challenged by a counter-argument in each body paragraph. The counter-argument is then refuted by a rebuttal in the same paragraph.

Exercise 5

Read the following model essay.

1. Which framework (A or B) does this essay use?

2. Circle the counter-argument(s) and underline the writer's rebuttal.

3. Complete the outline on page 67 for the essay.

Private Lessons: the Fastest Ticket to Fluency?

There are a number of ways to learn a foreign language. Students can study alone from a book, or go to a country where the language is spoken and learn while living there. For the majority of learners, however, taking a private or group language lesson is a natural choice. Some people believe that private lessons are a better way to acquire a language because they are more flexible and so can meet students' specific needs. However, in reality, group lessons are more effective for language learning because they allow students to learn from each other and provide a supportive atmosphere, both of which are vital in successful language acquisition.

First, it can be clearly seen that peer-learning, where students learn directly from each other, is essential to foreign language learning. It has been found that, in class environments, students learn mostly from their peers rather than from teachers (Raymond 25). For instance, in a group lesson, learners often do pair or group work. In this environment, they practice negotiating meaning, start and control discussions, and produce a wide variety of expressions (Raymond 30). All of these activities are widely believed to facilitate the acquisition of a foreign language, and group lessons offer chances to practice them with the help of their classmates.

Furthermore, it is apparent that a positive group atmosphere helps students to learn a foreign language. The most important condition for language learning is that the learner is not intimidated or exhausted. As Jordin, author of *Teaching a Language in Urban Areas*, indicates, group lessons are considerably less daunting or tiring for the average learner when there is no "non-stop spotlight of the instructor's attention" (40). Moreover, it is true that encouragement from peers is a "fabulous motivator," and friendship and a sense of support among students should not be underestimated (Johnson and Swinton 109). Learning a language can be a challenging experience for shy people. It also requires a great amount of endurance because language acquisition does not occur instantly. Therefore, knowing that there are others who are going through the same challenge can encourage students to continue their learning.

Those who are in favor of private lessons may argue that students can learn better in this style because they can "customize" their lessons. For example, a teacher and a student can set up a specific goal without thinking about other students' needs. However, it has been observed that at the beginner level, what students in group lessons learn is not different from that learned by students in private lessons (Johnson and Swinton 110). Another objection to group lessons may be that group learners have less opportunity to interact with teachers. While this is true, talking only with teachers does not necessarily create a desirable learning environment. According to a study which examined private language lessons, 70% of the conversation is dominated by the instructors (Wagner 128). In addition, because the majority of teacher talk consists of questions, it is common that the students do nothing but answer these questions in lessons (Horthorn 52). Such examples indicate that in private lessons, learners may not speak or use various communication skills as much as they would in group lessons. It is generally agreed that the most efficient way to acquire a language is to use it actively. Group lessons seem to realize this situation more effectively than private lessons.

In conclusion, although many people may believe that one-on-one lessons will lead to more effective language learning, examining the nature of group lessons proves otherwise. Learning in groups provides numerous opportunities to practice various skills which are essential in the acquisition of the target language. It also creates an atmosphere in which learners can feel more relaxed and receive encouragement from their peers. Moreover, the quality of learning in group lessons is no different from that of private lessons, but group lessons offer more opportunities to use the language in different situations. Many potential students choose group lessons considering only the costs; however, it seems clear that this choice is also wise in terms of effective learning.

Works Cited

Horthorn, Jack. "Immigration and Language Education." 25 Sep. 2005. Web. 1 Oct. 2005. <http://www.immigration/MOF/gov/jp>.

Johnson, Morgan and Barry Swinton. "Motivation and Environment in Classroom." *Pragmatics of Teaching* Mar. 1998: 44–56.

Jordin, Karen. *Teaching a Language in Urban Areas.* London: PIT, 1998.

Raymond, Lester. *Classroom Teaching.* Philadelphia: Abott, 2001.

Wagner, Patrick. "Discourse Analysis in ESL Classrooms." *ESL Current Issues* 7 Dec. 2006: 127–130.

OUTLINE

Thesis statement:

_____

_____

_____

Body paragraph 1
Topic sentence:

_____

_____

_____

Supporting points:

_____

_____

_____

Body paragraph 2
Topic sentence:

_____

_____

_____

Supporting points:

_____

_____

_____

Body paragraph 3
Counter-arguments:

_____

_____

_____

Rebuttals:

_____

_____

_____

The following part of a model essay on the same topic uses a different framework. Complete the outline on page 69.

Private Lessons: the Fastest Ticket to Fluency?

There are a number of ways to learn a foreign language. Students can study alone from a book, or go to a country where the language is spoken and learn while living there. For the majority of learners, however, taking private or group language lessons is a natural choice. Some people believe that private lessons are a better way to acquire a language because they are more flexible and so can meet students' specific needs. However, in reality, group lessons are more effective for language learning because they allow students to learn from each other, reduce the stress of the learning environment, and create a supportive atmosphere, all of which are vital in successful language acquisition.

First, there is evidence that peer-learning, or learning from other students, is essential in foreign language acquisition. Studies suggest that in class, students learn language mostly from their peers rather than from teachers (Raymond 25). In language classes, learners do pair or group work and practice negotiating meaning, start and control discussions, and produce a wide variety of expressions (Raymond 30). All of these activities are believed to efficiently facilitate the acquisition of a foreign language. Some people may argue that students can practice the same skills more effectively with teachers in private lessons. However, research indicates that most of the conversation in private lessons consists of teachers asking questions and students answering them (Horthorn 52). Since it is questionable that the skills mentioned above can be obtained successfully simply by answering questions, private lessons seem to fail in providing an environment in which learners can acquire the language competently.

Another advantage of group lessons is that it can create a less stressful atmosphere, which is also desirable in foreign language learning. To begin with, the most important condition for language learning is that the learner should not be intimidated or exhausted. While those who are against group lessons may insist that a teacher's being able to provide constant attention and support to a student is a significant advantage in private lessons, this may not always be true. According to *Teaching a Language in Urban Areas*, group lessons are considerably less daunting or tiring for the average learner because there is no "non-stop spotlight of the instructor's attention" (Jordin 40). This can be interpreted as meaning that group lessons are a desirable option for people who do not learn well in stressful situations.

In addition, the feeling of support which a learner can receive from their classmates is a valuable benefit which cannot be gained in private lessons ...

OUTLINE

Thesis statement:

_____

_____

_____

Body paragraph 1

Argument 1 (topic sentence):

There is evidence that peer-learning, learning from other students, is essential to foreign language acquisition.

Counter-argument 1:

A student can learn the skills needed to communicate in a target language more effectively from a teacher in private lessons.

Rebuttals to counter-argument:

From peer interaction, students learn various skills:

- negotiating meaning
- starting or controlling discussions
- using a variety of expressions

Body paragraph 2

Argument 2 (topic sentence):

_____

_____

_____

Counter-argument 2:

_____

_____

_____

Rebuttals to the counter-argument:

Group environment is:

- less daunting or tiring

- _____

- _____

Part

2 Organizing argumentative essays

Section 1   Introductory paragraph of an argumentative essay

As with all essay types, the introductory paragraph of an argumentative essay consists of three fundamental parts: a hook, building sentences, and a thesis statement.

1. Direct and indirect thesis statements

Section 1 on expository essays showed that the thesis statement in an essay can present the main ideas which support the writer's position on a topic. When the **main ideas are included** in the thesis statement, this is called a **direct thesis statement**. Direct thesis statements are effective in short essays with only two or three main ideas because they can all be clearly expressed in the thesis statement.

For essays of any length, an **indirect thesis statement** can be used. This type of thesis statement still presents the essay topic and the writer's position, but **includes only a summary of the main ideas** that will support the position in the essay. An indirect thesis requires the main ideas supporting the writer's position to be introduced in the building sentences.

Example of an indirect thesis statement:

<table>
<tr>
<td>

three main ideas to support the writer's position in the building sentences

</td>
<td>

There are a number of ways to learn a foreign language. Students can study alone from a book, or go to a country where the language is spoken and learn while living there. For the majority of learners, however, taking a private or group language lesson is a natural choice. Some people believe that private lessons are a better way to acquire a language because they are more flexible and so can meet students' specific needs. However, in reality, group lessons allow students to learn from each other, reduce the stress of the learning environment, and create a supportive atmosphere. Therefore, group lessons are more effective for language learning because the benefits derived from group interaction are vital to successful language acquisition.

</td>
</tr>
</table>

summary of main ideas in the thesis

Example of a direct thesis statement:

<table>
<tr>
<td>

three main ideas to support the writer's position in the thesis

</td>
<td>

There are a number of ways to learn a foreign language. Students can study alone from a book, or go to a country where the language is spoken and learn while living there. For the majority of learners, however, taking a private or group language lesson is a natural choice. Some people believe that private lessons are a better way to acquire a language because they are more flexible and so can meet students' specific needs. However, in reality, group lessons can provide benefits private lessons cannot. Group lessons are more effective for language learning because they allow students to learn from each other, reduce the stress of the learning environment, and create a supportive atmosphere.

</td>
</tr>
</table>

2. Introducing a counter-argument

In an argumentative essay, a counter-argument to the writer's argument needs to be included in the introductory paragraph. The counter-argument is placed before the thesis statement in the building sentences. The ideas that support the counter-argument will be introduced and developed in the body paragraphs using either framework A or B (pages 64).

Example:

counter-argument before the thesis

> There are a number of ways to learn a foreign language. Students can study alone from a book, or go to a country where the language is spoken and learn while living there. For the majority of learners, however, taking a private or group language lesson is a natural choice. Some people believe that private lessons are a better way to acquire a language because they are more flexible and so can meet students' specific needs. However, in reality, group lessons can provide benefits private lessons cannot. Group lessons are more effective for language learning because they allow students to learn from each other, reduce the stress of the learning environment, and create a supportive atmosphere.

Exercise 1

Read the following introductory paragraph from the model argumentative essay on pages 56–59, and answer the questions.

1. What thesis type is used?

2. What is the counter-argument?

The Democratizing of Knowledge: in Defense of Wikipedia

As the internet gained popularity, many hoped it would develop as a decentralizing and democratizing force where people could share information and learn from each other. Wikipedia, a free online encyclopedia and the world's largest reference resource, embodies such ideals in allowing multiple users to write and revise content. This collaborative practice differs from the process of compiling conventional encyclopedias, which relies on scholars and experts to contribute information. Wikipedia's underlying belief is that by having more participants contributing and editing information, each entry will have greater range, depth, and accuracy. Some, however, claim such thinking is naive and fundamentally flawed due to the belief that a reliance on amateur editors will lead to inaccurate and unreliable entries. Yet, Wikipedia does provide a useful starting point for research, offering a comprehensive overview of complex topics, a neutral editorial stance, and a dedicated commitment to quality.

Exercise 2

Rewrite the above introductory paragraph using a different thesis type.

_____

_____

_____

_____

_____

_____

_____

_____

_____

_____

_____

_____

_____

_____

_____

_____

The body paragraphs of an argumentative essay follow the same organization as body paragraphs in an expository essay (topic sentence, supporting sentences, and concluding sentence). In addition, ideas are developed using the **reason–evidence–explanation waltz method**.

Within this structure, the following elements are essential for developing logical arguments:

- phrases to introduce an argument.
- transitional expressions.
- support from outside sources.

1. Phrases to introduce an argument

In an argumentative essay, certain phrases are commonly used to introduce arguments, counter-arguments, and rebuttals.

Arguments can be introduced with the impersonal *it* followed by a clause.

Phrase	Example
It is clear that …	**It is clear that** *language cannot be acquired without using it.*
It can be argued that … *demonstrated* *clearly seen*	**It can be argued that** *there is no sharp distinction between tutored learning and untutored learning.*
It seems (likely) that …	**It seems likely that** *a third language is easier to learn after mastering a second one.*

Arguments can also be introduced with *there* followed by a clause.

Phrase	Example
There is no doubt that … *little question*	**There is no doubt that** *motivation plays a significant role in adult language learners.*
There is evidence to demonstrate *indicate* *suggest* *that …*	**There is evidence to suggest that** *the size of vocabulary seriously affects listening ability.*
There is a great deal of research which demonstrates that …	**There is a great deal of research which demonstrates that** *the process of language acquisition is different in adults and children.*

Exercise 3   Read the model essay on pages 56–59 and underline phrases that introduce arguments.

Exercise 4   Rewrite the following statements by using the phrases to introduce arguments.

1. Language students should train themselves to think as native speakers.

    _____

    _____

2. Infants' brains are said to have the ability to acquire a limitless number of languages.

    _____

    _____

3. Bilingualism is difficult to achieve without proper instruction.

    _____

    _____

4. Foreign languages cannot be acquired effectively when learners are not motivated.

    _____

    _____

5. The speed of language learning increases when learners are given tasks slightly above their current level of ability.

    _____

    _____

2. Transitional expressions

Transitional expressions are words and phrases which show the relationship between ideas. They are important for creating a logical flow, known as **cohesion**, in an essay. By using transitional expressions effectively, the writer can show whether the writing will continue with a similar idea, introduce an opposite idea, show an example, or conclude. Transitional expressions are normally followed by a comma.

Transitional expressions	Function	Sample sentences
first, second *first of all* *finally*	To list ideas	*__First__, it can be clearly seen that peer-learning, where students learn directly from each other, is essential to foreign language learning.*
also *moreover* *furthermore* *in addition (to …)* *another*	To add an idea	*According to a study which examined private language lessons, 70% of conversation is dominated by the instructors. __In addition__, because the majority of teacher talk consists of questions, it is common that the students do nothing but answer these questions in lessons.*
however *in contrast* *on the other hand* *in spite of …* *although*	To introduce a contrasting idea	*There are a number of ways to learn a foreign language. Students can study alone from a book, or go to a country where the language is spoken and learn while living there. __However__, the majority of learners take language lessons.*
for example *for instance*	To show an example	*It has been found that, in class environments, students learn mostly from their peers rather than from teachers. __For instance__, in group lessons, learners often do pair or group work. In this environment, they practice negotiating meaning, start and control discussions, and produce a wide variety of expressions.*
therefore *accordingly* *consequently* *as a result* *due to …* *because of …*	To state an effect or result	*It is said that non-native speakers will soon outnumber native speakers of English. __Therefore__, learners are far more likely to use English with non-native speakers in the future.*
otherwise	To give an alternative consequence	*Some parents believe that children should start learning a foreign language as early as possible. __Otherwise__, acquiring native like fluency will become increasingly difficult.*
in other words	To restate an idea given in the previous sentence	*It is suggested that young children possess metalinguistic awareness. __In other words__, children are conscious of how they learn when acquiring more than one language at a time.*

Exercise 5   **Fill in the blanks with appropriate transitional expressions. More than one answer is possible for some of the sentences.**

1. Although there are an estimated 1.3 to 1.5 billion English speakers in the world, native speakers constitute well below half that amount. _____ the majority of people who speak English are non-native speakers.

2. Along with English, Welsh is an official language in Wales. _____ only 25% of the population speak it fluently.

3. English is considered to be the global language of business. _____ many business people in non-English speaking countries want to learn it.

4. Many words in English are derived from Greek. _____ *idea*, *economy*, and *gym* all have their origin in this language.

5. In the language classroom in which the Direct Method is adopted, learners' mother language should never be used. _____, the teacher in this classroom needs to use pictures and gestures to convey meaning.

3. Improving paragraph-to-paragraph cohesion

Well-linked paragraphs improve cohesion in the essay. One way to achieve this is to use certain transitional words and phrases in the topic sentence of each body paragraph.

In the following example, transitional expressions are used to clearly indicate how the topic sentences of the body paragraphs are linked to the main ideas supporting the thesis of an essay.

Thesis statement:

Group lessons are more effective for language learning because they allow students to learn from each other, reduce the stress of the learning environment, and create a supportive atmosphere.

Using transitional *words*

Body paragraph 1 topic sentence:
First, it can be clearly seen that peer-learning, where students learn directly from each other, is essential to foreign language acquisition.

Body paragraph 2 topic sentence:
Moreover, it can be argued that group lessons provide a less stressful environment, which results in more effective language learning.

Body paragraph 3 topic sentence:
Finally, learners in group lessons can receive support not only from their teacher but also from their classmates.

Using transitional *phrases*

Body paragraph 1 topic sentence:
To begin with, it can be clearly seen that peer-learning, where students learn directly from each other, is essential to foreign language acquisition.

Body paragraph 2 topic sentence:
In addition, it can be argued that group lessons provide a less stressful environment, which results in more effective language learning.

Body paragraph 3 topic sentence:
Another advantage of group lessons is that learners in group lessons can receive support not only from their teacher but also from their classmates.

Using a combination of transitional *words* and *phrases*

Body paragraph 1 topic sentence:
First, it can be clearly seen that peer-learning, where students learn directly from each other, is essential to foreign language acquisition.

Body paragraph 2 topic sentence:
Another advantage of group lessons is that they provide a less stressful environment, which results in more effective language learning.

Body paragraph 3 topic sentence:
Finally, in addition to learning from peers and being in a less stressful environment, learners in group lessons can receive encouragement from their classmates.

Exercise 6 **Read the following part of an essay and fill in the blanks with appropriate transitional expressions. Sometimes more than one answer is possible.**

Early Foreign Language Education

Starting more than three decades ago, learning English has steadily become one of the most common free-time activities for non-native speaking English people of all ages. _____ busy business people may attend late night classes, or the elderly often attend group lessons as a social activity. Young children have also started to learn English. _____ 30% of parents of preschool-aged children said they had plans to enroll their children in English schools ("Parental"). _____ some parents have sent their children to middle or high schools overseas in an effort to give them a head start on a glamorous international career. _____ many people believe in the promise of an early English education, starting at too early an age can create problems. Studying English at a young age can lead to low achievement in native as well as foreign language acquisition and also lead to cultural identification difficulties in children …

_____ teaching young children English should require more caution because it can negatively affect their acquisition of both native and foreign languages. _____ many researchers suggest that if children are totally immersed in a foreign language before they acquire the basic rules and structures of their mother tongue, it might limit their learning of the foreign language at the advanced level (Saddler 155). _____ if learners use a foreign language primarily at the critical ages for learning native language, it would hamper their native language development …

Proponents of early foreign language education argue that language is most effectively learned when learners are young. _____ the Critical Period Hypothesis in foreign language acquisition advocates that people learn the sounds of language best before the age of six, or before puberty (Johnson and Newport 70). _____ there is a great deal of research which demonstrates that learners who started learning as a college student can also acquire the correct sounds of a target language if they are in the proper environment (Wiley 216). _____ early foreign language education is not necessary because it can harm one's acquisition of both native and foreign languages, and the second language can be learned well after the establishment of the first language. _____ teaching young children English can make them feel confused about their cultural identities …

4. Support from outside sources

The following kinds of information should be used to provide convincing support for the writer's opinion:

- authoritative opinions.
- specific examples.
- statistical evidence.

Authoritative opinions

An effective way to strengthen the writer's argument is to use **evidence from respected authorities** (experts) on the essay topic, such as academics or well-known writers.

Example:

Researchers at Dartmouth College concluded that these large numbers and the rules for contribution indicate that Wikipedia users are accessing information which is constantly being updated and checked for errors, therefore ensuring the information is accurate, which is a feature not available with traditional encyclopedias.

Specific examples

Specific examples are also effective in supporting the writer's argument as they **help to explain an idea** simply and clearly.

Example:

Wikipedia's policy also ensures that neutrality is maintained, which is crucial for academic research on issues which are fiercely contested. For example, globalization issues involve pro-globalization and anti-globalization arguments, but both sides are described comprehensively in the Wikipedia entry on the topic.

Statistical evidence

Statistics can also be used as evidence and are a direct way of **proving the validity** of the writer's argument.

Example:

Wikipedia is not exclusive to those who can read English. One of the most frequented websites in the world, it is also a multilingual resource with 270 non-English Wikipedia sites ("User-generated").

5. Concluding sentences in body paragraphs

Just as with expository essays, paragraphs in argumentative essays with multiple reasons supporting the topic sentence may need a concluding sentence to:

- summarize the reasons in the paragraph.
- show how the reasons prove the writer's position in the thesis.

Paragraphs should not end with outside information, such as quotations, summaries, or paraphrases. The final sentence should always present the essay writer's own thoughts.

Examples:

✗ *Wikipedia's value is also evident in the breadth of information available. Olivia Solon, news editor at Wired.co.uk states that Wikipedia carries over 3.5 million entries across a diverse variety of topics ranging from the technical to the trivial. Furthermore, Wikipedia features hyperlinks within entries to related topics/terms, providing users with direct access to additional sources which may lead to a deeper understanding of a topic. Moreover, Wikipedia is not exclusive to those who can read English. One of the most frequented websites in the world, it is also a multilingual resource with 270 non-English Wikipedia sites ("User-generated").*

Paragraph ends with outside information.	

✓ *Wikipedia's value is also evident in the breadth of information available. Olivia Solon, news editor at Wired.co.uk states that Wikipedia carries over 3.5 million entries across a diverse variety of topics ranging from the technical to the trivial. Furthermore, Wikipedia features hyperlinks within entries to related topics/terms, providing users with direct access to additional sources which may lead to a deeper understanding of a topic. Moreover, Wikipedia is not exclusive to those who can read English: not only is it one of the most frequented websites in the world, but it is also a multilingual resource with 270 non-English Wikipedia sites ("User-generated"). The result is a website which is a useful "one-stop" resource for research across disciplines and languages. The success of Wikipedia, therefore, has democratized knowledge through its vast amount of accurate and up-to-date information, and through its belief that any responsible user or contributor can access and add knowledge for the benefit of all people.*

Paragraph ends with the writer's thought.	

As with other types of essays, the concluding paragraph of an argumentative essay:

- restates the thesis statement.
- summarizes the main points (including counter-arguments and rebuttals).
- finishes with the writer's final thought.

The conclusion should leave the reader with the feeling that the writer's argument is complete and that its implications have been fully considered.

The following concluding paragraph is from the model essay on pages 56–59.

restatement of the thesis

summary of the main points

writer's final thought

To conclude, Wikipedia, with its breadth, depth, and reliability, serves as an excellent starting point for researchers of virtually any topic. It features millions of entries across a wide range of topics which are updated constantly. Researchers can confidently turn to it for comprehensive and mostly unbiased information on even the most complex and controversial of topics. While some fear that having too many contributors will lead to inaccurate and even harmful content, measures to ensure that the quality of the entries is maintained have allowed Wikipedia to achieve a level of accuracy close to that of other, more conventional encyclopedias. Though not perfect, Wikipedia has demonstrated that the potential of the internet to decentralize sources of information and empower people can be achieved.

3 Improving your work

Section 1   Avoiding overgeneralization

Overgeneralization describes a statement which is inaccurately presented as being true in all situations:

People believe that Wikipedia is an unreliable source of information since anybody can write and revise its content.

This sentence means that all people believe that Wikipedia is an unreliable source of information. Clearly, there may be people who do not believe this. Overgeneralization gives the impression that the writer is unaware of, or has not considered other possibilities. This makes the writer's arguments appear weak and less convincing to the reader.

Overgeneralization can be avoided by the use of **hedging** terms:

Many *people* ***seem*** *to believe that Wikipedia is an unreliable source of information since anybody can write and revise its content.*

Examples of language used in hedging:

Verbs: *seem, tend, appear, indicate, suggest, assume, believe*

Modal verbs: *may, might, can, could*

Adjectives: *many, some, few*

Adverbs of frequency: *usually, often, sometimes*

Adverbs of certainty: *probably, possibly, perhaps, conceivably*

Nouns: *assumption, possibility, probability*

Exercise 1   Circle the hedging expressions in the model essay on pages 56–59.

Section 2   Avoiding redundancy

A word or phrase is considered redundant when it is needlessly repeated. To avoid redundancy, look out for the following:

* repetition of vocabulary or phrases in sentences and paragraphs.
* sentences within a paragraph that have the same meaning.
* paragraphs in an essay where the main ideas are too related to each other.

In these examples, the underlined parts need to be changed to avoid redundancy:

✗ *The <u>basic fundamentals</u> of successful language learning are motivation and practice.*

✓ *The fundamentals of successful language learning are motivation and practice.*

✗ *If students do not understand, the teacher will <u>repeat</u> the question <u>again</u>.*

✓ *If students do not understand, the teacher will repeat the question.*

✗ *One benefit of studying abroad is that one can experience a country's language and culture directly. <u>People are more exposed to the language and culture by living in the country</u>.*

✓ *One benefit of studying abroad is that one can experience a country's language and culture directly.*

<table>
<tr><td>Exercise 2</td><td>**In the following paragraph, identify the redundant sentences and delete them.**</td></tr>
</table>

A native English speaker's judgment on the ability of a language learner often depends on pronunciation. Good pronunciation makes a speaker sound fluent in the language. Thus, if learners wish to be regarded as fluent, they need to practice pronunciation, not grammar. Focusing on pronunciation helps more than studying structure and words. Can a non-native speaker talk like a native English speaker without knowledge of grammar and a large vocabulary? Theoretically it is possible because native speakers do not always talk grammatically and may often use words incorrectly. Native speakers make grammar mistakes and may use only limited vocabulary. However, if students wish to achieve an advanced level of English, naturally, they need to have more than good pronunciation. Good pronunciation is not enough to make a non-native speaker an effective user of the language.

Section 3   Avoiding vague or "empty" words

Some words, such as *important, interesting, bad,* and *good* are too general or vague. These words often weaken the intended meaning of a sentence because they make the reader guess what the writer means, which may be inaccurate.

In the sentence that follows, the word *important* is unclear because all languages, not just English, are important in some way. As a result, the entire sentence has almost no meaning:

✗ *English is an <u>important</u> language in the the world.*

The meaning of a sentence using words such as *important*, *interesting*, *bad*, and *good* can be clarified in two ways:

- by providing a reason why something is *important*, *interesting*, *bad*, or *good*.
- by replacing the word with another word or phrase that has a more specific meaning.

Examples:

✓ *English is an **important** language in the world **because it has become the language of international communication**.*

✓ *English is a **necessary** language **to know** because it has become the language of international communication.*

In addition, words and expressions which do not change or add to the meaning of a sentence are considered "*empty*." These words and expressions should simply be removed.

Examples:

✗ *The linguist Barry McLaughlin is <u>a</u> widely respected <u>person</u>.*

✓ *The linguist Barry McLaughlin is widely respected.*

✗ <u>*The experience of*</u> *learning English can often be difficult and time-consuming.*

✓ *Learning English can often be difficult and time-consuming.*

Exercise 3

Rewrite the following sentences improving any vague or empty expressions.

1. An English learner's native language is the one that influences their learning most.

2. Each language has a set of good phrases to express sympathy and gratitude.

3. Maintaining students' motivation is an important thing for teachers.

4. At all times, language teaching can be a difficult job.

5. Selected texts, if good, can motivate students to read more and increase their reading speed.

In addition to the points presented in Unit 1, Part 3, consider the following extra points when revising an argumentative essay.

First draft checklist

Whole essay

1. Is the essay an appropriate length?
2. Is the tone of writing objective?
3. Is the writer's argument clear and logical?
4. After reading counter-arguments and rebuttals, is the argument still strong?

Introductory paragraph

5. Is there a "hook"? Does the hook make the reader want to continue reading?
6. Do the building sentences lead logically to the thesis statement?
7. Is a counter-argument stated clearly?
8. If a direct thesis statement is used, does it clearly state the writer's position and introduce the topics of each body paragraph?
9. If an indirect thesis statement is used, are the main ideas supporting the writer's position expressed in the building sentences, and are they summarized in the thesis?

Body paragraphs

10. Does the topic sentence show the topic and controlling idea of the paragraph?
11. Do the supporting sentences logically support the topic sentence?
12. Are there enough details to support the topics in each body paragraph?
13. Do the citations make the writer's argument stronger?

Counter-arguments and rebuttals

14. Are the counter-arguments relevant to the essay topic?
15. Does each rebuttal focus directly on one counter-argument?
16. Does each rebuttal present a logical refutation of that counter-argument?

Concluding paragraph

17. Is the thesis restated?
18. Is there a summary of each main idea in the body paragraphs?
19. Is there a final thought? Does the essay feel "completed" by this?
20. Are new ideas avoided in this paragraph?

Language/coherence

21. Are the writer's arguments, counter-arguments, and rebuttals clearly introduced?
22. Are appropriate transitional expressions used to connect sentence and paragraph ideas?
23. Are overgeneralization, redundancy, emptiness, and vagueness avoided?

Exercise 4   Edit the following essay draft using the checklist on page 86.

Multilingualism

If you have traveled in Europe, you must have noticed that many people there are multilingual. If you happen to be struggling to acquire a second language, you must certainly have felt envious of this European situation. Besides, Europe is a wonderful place to visit! Some researchers advocate that multilinguals are better language learners than monolinguals or bilinguals. They also say that children should start learning as many foreign languages as early as possible. It is said that the benefits of multilingualism are many.

First of all, learning multiple languages requires students to look for similarities among the languages that they already know and the one they are learning. As a result, learning a new language enables them to "reactivate" their knowledge of the other languages (Jessner 201). Thus, learning another language can strengthen a learner's overall language skills. Languages are basically creations of the human brain; thus there should be similarities among the languages. Even though the ways to express human thoughts are numerous, we share our thoughts with other people living in different regions of the world. Realization of similarities leads us to world peace.

In a comparative study of bilingual and monolingual children, it has been pointed out that children begin to recognize how they acquire languages in the process of learning multiple numbers of languages. This recognition is called "metalinguistic awareness" (Jessner 201). It seems that metalinguistic awareness is the work of a highly functioning brain. Studies indicate that successful bilinguals develop better cognitive skills than monolingual children (Baker 31). It was found that there are differences between the thought process of trilingual adults and monolingual adults. Therefore, the knowledge of extra languages can enhance learners' cognitive ability.

As the world is getting smaller, the skills of multiple languages certainly help us to promote international economy, politics, and culture. Practically speaking, it seems that multilinguals tend to get higher class jobs compared to monolinguals and bilinguals. Also, Collier said that multilinguals are creative and think divergently.

Some people may disagree with multilingualism. They would argue that learning more languages may cause confusion among learners.

It has been said that the linguistic ability that our brain can handle is not limitless and everyone has the same limited ability. So if one person learns several languages, each language would be weak and they may not have one perfect language. However, this is not true as I said earlier. Moreover, some researchers said that learning two or more languages which are very much different from each other, such as English and Japanese, will make your brain function better since the learning may use different parts of the brain.

In conclusion, the benefit of multilingualism is more than the simply knowledge of multiple languages; learning different languages makes the learners learn beyond the languages themselves. I do not like being monolingual. Since there are many benefits of becoming multilingual, I would like to acquire more than two languages. However, the system in my country seems to be behind Western's. This is probably because people in my country do not see the whole wide world. This is a terrible situation for me and my friends. So I suggest that the government spend more to improve the level of our school language classes. They should start today!

Works Cited

Baker, Colin. *Foundations of Bilingual Education and Bilingualism.* Clevedon: Multilingual Matters. 1996.

Collier, Virginea P. "A Synthesis of Studies Examining Long-term Language Minority Student Data on Academic Achievement." *Bilingual Research Journal* 16 (1992): 187–212.

Jessner, Ulrike. "Metalinguistic Awareness in Multilinguals: Cognitive Aspects of Third Language learning." *Language Awareness* VoL. 8: 3 & 4 (1999): 201–209.

UNIT 4

Writing a Compare and Contrast Essay

P a r t

1 Compare and contrast essay structure

Section 1 Starting a compare and contrast essay

A compare and contrast essay examines two or more subjects to establish **the degree of similarity** (compare) or **difference** (contrast) between them. The overall goal of this type of essay is to gain a deeper understanding of both subjects. Therefore, when writing a compare and contrast essay, each subject must be written about with equal detail.

Compare and contrast essays also have specific goals. They can either:

• explain the similarities, differences, or both between the subjects in detail, or
• make an argument about the similarities, differences, or both between the subjects.

The pre-writing steps for a compare and contrast essay are as follows:

1. Read the essay question and establish a **reason for comparison**.
2. Read sources and decide the **points of comparison**.
3. Write a thesis statement.
4. Select an essay pattern.
5. Outline the essay.

1. Establish a reason for comparison

As in all essays, a compare and contrast essay requires a motive. In a compare and contrast essay, the motive is expressed by the **reason for comparison**. Two subjects can often be compared and contrasted for many reasons. The reason for comparison indicates why the subjects are being compared. Having a specific reason for comparison gives the essay a purpose, and will help guide the research required to write the essay. The reason for comparison is often stated in the essay question.

Compare the following examples:

Example question 1
Compare and contrast <u>how students are educated</u> in public and home schools.

reason for comparison

Example question 2
Compare and contrast public and home schools. <u>Which system prepares students for university more effectively</u>?

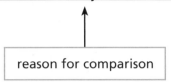

reason for comparison

Both questions ask the writer to compare home schools and public schools. However, the reasons for comparison are different between the two questions. This difference will result in a different approach in the essay. In question 1, the goal of the essay will be only to explain the similarities, differences, or both between public and home schools in terms of "how students are educated." In question 2, the goal of the essay will be to use the similarities, differences, or both between the subjects in order to argue which method of education better "prepares students for university."

Sometimes a question does not include a reason for comparison. In this type of question, the essay writer must consider a reason based on their research or knowledge of both subjects.

Example question 3
Compare and contrast public and private schools in your country.

In the above question, only the two subjects to be compared are given, so the essay writer must decide the reason for comparison. For example, the writer may wish to compare and/or contrast:

- the difficulty of academics and courses.
- the students who attend.
- the resources provided.

After deciding the reason for comparison the essay writer can also choose the goal of the essay: to explain, or to argue.

Exercise 1

Write two possible reasons for comparison for the following items.

Example: Tea and coffee

which is better for health – drinking tea or drinking coffee

the role that tea and coffee houses play in society

1. Movies and books

_____

_____

2. Team sports and individual sports

_____

_____

3. Studying at a university in your own country and studying abroad

_____

_____

2. Choose points of comparison

After establishing a reason for comparison between the two subjects, the writer needs to choose **points of comparison**. These points must be related to the reason for comparison.

Example question 1:
Compare and contrast how students are educated in public and home schools.

Possible points of comparison:
* curriculum.
* teachers.
* other students.

Curriculum, teachers, and other students have a significant effect on how students are educated at both types of schools, so using them as points of comparison would effectively answer the essay prompt.

Example question 3:
Compare and contrast public and private schools in your country.

If the writer chooses "the students who attend" as the reason for comparison, possible points of comparison are:
* class size.
* intelligence.
* background.

Class size, intelligence, and background would be legitimate points of comparison because they are all related to the students who attend public and private schools.

Exercise 2

Using the answers from Exercise 1, list three possible points of comparison.

1. Movies and books

Reason for comparison 1:	Reason for comparison 2:
_____	_____
Points:	Points:
_____	_____
_____	_____
_____	_____

2. Team sports and individual sports

Reason for comparison 1: Points: _____ _____ _____	Reason for comparison 2: Points: _____ _____ _____

3. Studying at a university in your own country and studying abroad

Reason for comparison 1: Points: _____ _____ _____	Reason for comparison 2: Points: _____ _____ _____

3. Write a thesis statement

As in other essays, the thesis statement of a compare and contrast essay should tell readers what the essay is about and what they can expect to read in the body. Specifically, the thesis statement of a compare and contrast essay should contain:

• the two subjects being compared or contrasted.

• their relationship: similar, different, or both.

• the reason for comparison.

• the points of comparison.

From the Example question 1 on page 92, one possible thesis is:

How students are educated in public and home schools is quite different in terms of the curriculum, quality of teaching, and the presence of other students.

The essential parts of this thesis are:

• the two subjects – *public and home school.*

• their relationship – *different.*

• the reason for comparison – *how students are educated.*

• the points of comparison – *curriculum, quality of teaching, and the presence of other students.*

Using one of the reasons for comparison and its points of comparison from Exercise 2, write a possible thesis statement for each.

1. Movies and books

   _____

   _____

   _____

2. Team sports and individual sports

   _____

   _____

   _____

3. Studying at a university in your own country and studying abroad

   _____

   _____

   _____

4. Select an essay pattern

The introductory paragraph, the body paragraphs, and the concluding paragraph in a compare and contrast essay follow the same organization as other essays.

The introductory paragraph, has:

- a hook.
- building sentences.
- a thesis.

The body paragraphs have:

- a topic sentence.
- supporting sentences organized using the "waltz".
- a concluding sentence (if necessary).

The concluding paragraph has:

- a restated thesis.
- a summary of the points of comparison.
- a final thought.

However, in the body paragraphs, compare and contrast essays can have one of two patterns: either **subject by subject** or **point by point**.

Pattern 1: subject by subject

In a subject-by-subject pattern, there are **only two body paragraphs**.

Public Schools and Home Schools

1. Introductory paragraph

2. Body paragraph 1: Public school
    A. Curriculum
    B. Teachers
    C. Other students

3. Body paragraph 2: Home school
    A. Curriculum
    B. Teachers
    C. Other students

4. Concluding paragraph

Points to keep in mind regarding this pattern:
- In the first body paragraph, the first subject is explained in detail.
- In the second body paragraph, the second subject is explained in detail with comparisons and contrasts to the first subject.
- The points of comparison should be the same in both body paragraphs and should be presented in the same order.
- This pattern is more appropriate for shorter essays with fewer points of comparison.

Pattern 2: point by point

In longer essays with more points of comparison, the point-by-point pattern allows the reader to focus on the points being compared more easily. **Each body paragraph** is focused on comparing and contrasting **one point of comparison** between the two subjects. This pattern is appropriate for either shorter or longer essays.

Public Schools and Home Schools

1. Introductory paragraph

2. Body paragraph 1: **Curriculum**
   Similarities and/or differences between public schools and home schools

3. Body paragraph 2: **Teachers**
   Similarities and/or differences between public schools and home schools

4. Body paragraph 3: **Other students**
   Similarities and/or differences between public schools and home schools

5. Concluding paragraph

Exercise 4

Read the sample essays A and B on pages 98–101, and identify which pattern is used in each.

5. Outline the essay

After choosing a pattern, outline your essay. When outlining a compare and contrast essay, list the details for each point of comparison between the two subjects next to each other on a table. The following example outline is for an essay with this thesis:

How students are educated in public and home schools is quite different in terms of the curriculum, quality of teaching, and the presence of other students.

Point of comparison	Public	Home school
Curriculum	• Regulated by government • Must be appropriate for a diverse group of students	• Lack regulation • Possible to structure curriculum based on student level, interests, etc.
Teachers	• Certified • More than one – variety of specialties	• Not certified (usually a parent) • Single teacher – more personal attention for student
Other students	• More students – opportunities for diverse social interactions • Group work and exchange of ideas helps learning	• More limited social interactions – planned/ controlled by parents • Student can move at a pace suited to own abilities, interests

Exercise 5

Using the points of comparison from Exercise 2 (pages 92–93), make an outline for the following:

1. Movies and books

2. Team sports and individual sports

3. Studying at a university in your own country and studying abroad

Educating Students in Public and Home Schools

One of the top concerns of parents is their children's education. Yet, how and where they can receive the best quality education remains open to debate. In the United States, traditional public schools remain the common choice for most parents, but a growing number are choosing to school their children in their own homes. Officially, both school options must follow the same educational guidelines established by their respective state. Having these guidelines suggests that students study in similar ways in each school environment. However, the guidelines only set goals for students, so the methods each form of education adopts to reach these goals can vary considerably. How students are educated in public schools and home schools is quite different in terms of the curriculum, quality of teaching, and in the interaction with other students.

When looking at public schools, aspects of their educational environments are determined by the fact that they are public institutions with a diversity of students. One of these aspects is the curriculum. Along with core courses in language, math, and science, broad-ranging courses such as history, geography, music, physical education, and social studies are offered in order to provide a comprehensive education (Bielick 4). This variety in courses serves to expose students to a wide range of subjects, thereby giving them a chance to discover which subjects might be of particular interest. Moreover, public schools must monitor and report to education officials on the effectiveness of the curriculum (Ravitch 10). This ensures that the quality of the curriculum is maintained and that goals are reached. Additionally, the teachers themselves are crucial in public education. American College Testing (ACT) argues that along with their specialized course knowledge and educational training, the variety in teachers' styles and personalities can stimulate students and foster a deeper appreciation for subjects in both interested students, and in students who may not even enjoy the subject ("Benefits" 2). Considering the number of courses offered during the years of school education, changing teachers regularly can be an enriching experience for students. A third critical aspect in public school education is the students themselves. Romanowski points out that public school students routinely exchange ideas and work together in groups. While they may not always like each other, they learn to adapt and cope with the diversity of backgrounds, values, and experience present among students in a public school class (82). This facilitates a type of learning beyond what books or even a teacher can provide, but which forms an essential element in learning to live in a diverse society. In short, diversity seems to be a major asset found in the public school educational environment.

Home schools, however, offer a contrasting education environment to public schools due to the more private nature of their learning environment. The curriculum in home schools, for instance, is much more flexible than in public schools. Despite having to officially teach the same curriculum as public schools, most states in the U.S. have fewer regulations for home schools ("Homeschooling Thru"). This lack of regulation led to a *New York Times* report that found the majority of home schools do not submit any information to local school officials (*Homeschooling Regulations*). While some critics may argue that it is more likely for students in home schools to be deprived of a diverse education, many home school advocates believe that a less regulated curriculum allows it to be shaped according to the interests and skill level of individual students, thereby making it more educationally beneficial to the student. Furthermore, as the curriculum at home schools is less regulated than in public schools, so too are teachers at home schools. Home school teachers require no special teacher training or expertise in all of the subjects taught, which leads to criticism over the qualification of these teachers to actually teach (Romanowski 80). However, it can be argued that the personal attention a student in a home school receives leads to better academic performance than can be achieved with a certified teacher teaching a class with a large number of students. Lastly, perhaps one of the most significant contrasts between public and home schools is the society of other students. While home school students can interact with each other via the internet and even participate in occasional field trips, they generally spend their day alone with a parent, or in some cases, a small group ("Homeschooling Thru"). Although this prevents them from experiencing the diversity to be found in public schools, it is a situation some parents prefer. In her report for the National Center for Education Statistics, for example, Bielick found that almost 75% of parents chose to home-school their children for religious or moral reasons (2). This suggests that home-schooled students are purposely kept apart from others to ensure only family beliefs are taught, or even to prevent them from being negatively influenced by classmates. In all, therefore, homeschooling has become an option for those who relate quality of education with flexibility and personal attention – aspects which give teachers, often a parent, more control in shaping the learning experience of their student.

In conclusion, public and home schools have contrasting attributes which result in different educational styles and benefits. In public schools, more regulated learning and more diversity in the curriculum, teachers, and students can be expected. Many people see this as important in preparing students for later life. Home schools, on the other hand, are less regulated and thereby offer parents the opportunity to exercise greater control over what their children are learning and with whom they are socializing. These considerable differences between public and home schools mean that parents will have to assess their own definition of quality education if they are considering either option for their children.

Educating Students in Public and Home Schools

One of the top concerns of parents is their children's education. Yet, how and where they can receive the best quality education remains open to debate. In the United States, traditional public schools remain the common choice for most parents, but a growing number are choosing to school their children in their own homes. Officially, both school options must follow the same educational guidelines established by their respective state. Having these guidelines suggests that students study in similar ways in each school environment. However, the guidelines only set goals for students, so the methods each form of education adopts to reach these goals can vary considerably. How students are educated in public schools and home schools is quite different in terms of the curriculum, quality of teaching, and in the interaction with other students.

One of the major differences between public and home schools affecting how students are educated is the curriculum. Public school curriculums are designed around serving a diverse range of students with diverse interests. Along with core courses in language, math, and science, broad-ranging courses such as history, geography, music, physical education, and social studies are offered in order to provide a comprehensive education (Bielick 4). This variety in courses serves to expose students to a wide range of subjects, thereby giving them a chance to discover which subjects might be of particular interest. Moreover, public schools must monitor and report to education officials on the effectiveness of the curriculum (Ravitch 10). This ensures that the quality of the curriculum is maintained and that goals are reached. The curriculum in home schools, however, is much more flexible than in public schools. Despite having to officially teach the same curriculum as public schools, most states in the U.S. have fewer regulations for home schools ("Homeschooling Thru"). This lack of regulation led to a *New York Times* report that found the majority of home schools do not submit any information to local school officials (*Homeschooling Regulations*). While some critics may argue that it is more likely for students in home schools to be deprived of a diverse education, many home school advocates believe that a less regulated curriculum allows it to be shaped according to the interests and skill level of individual students, thereby making it more educationally beneficial to the student. Therefore, parents considering the best type of education for their children need to consider whether a curriculum's diversity or flexibility should be given priority.

While the curriculum is important, the teachers of the curriculum are also a key factor in determining how students learn. In public schools, having teachers who are not only certified but specialized in particular subjects is seen as an asset. American College Testing (ACT) argues that along with their specialized course knowledge and educational training, the variety in teachers' styles and personalities can stimulate students and foster a deeper appreciation for subjects in both interested students and in students who may not even enjoy the subject ("Benefits" 2). Considering the number of courses offered during the years of school education, changing teachers regularly can be an enriching experience for students in public schools. Most home school teachers, however, are the only teacher for a particular student, and often this teacher is the student's parent and not certified as a teacher. Home school teachers require no special teacher training or expertise in all of the subjects taught, which leads to criticism over the qualification of these teachers to actually teach (Romanowski 80). However, it can be argued that the personal attention a student in a home school receives leads to better academic performance than can be achieved by a certified teacher teaching a class with a large number of students. Assessing the teaching situation in public and home schools, then, is another crucial consideration for parents seeking the ideal learning opportunity for their children.

A third critical aspect differentiating the education in public and home schools is the presence of other students. In public schools, student populations are often large and diverse, which some see as a major asset. Romanowski points out that public school students routinely exchange ideas and work together in groups. While they may not always like each other, they learn to adapt and cope with the diversity of backgrounds, values, and experience present among students in a public school class (82). This facilitates a type of learning beyond what books or even a teacher can provide, but which forms an essential element in learning to live in a diverse society. On the other hand, students in home schools are in a very different situation. While home school students can interact with each other via the internet and even participate in occasional field trips, they generally spend their day alone with a parent, or in some cases, a small group. ("Homeschooling Thru"). Although this prevents them from experiencing the diversity to be found in public schools, it is a situation some parents prefer. In her report for the National Center for Education Statistics, Bielick found that almost 75% of parents chose to home-school their children for religious or moral reasons (2). This suggests that home-schooled students are purposely kept apart from others to ensure only family beliefs are taught, or even to prevent them from being negatively influenced by classmates. Therefore, when weighing quality of education in public versus home schools, parents must decide whether the presence of other students is a benefit or drawback.

In conclusion, public and home schools have contrasting attributes which result in different educational styles and benefits. In public schools, more regulated learning and more diversity in the curriculum, teachers, and students can be expected. Many people see this as important in preparing students for later life. Home schools, on the other hand, are less regulated and thereby offer parents the opportunity to exercise greater control over what their children are learning and with whom they are socializing. These considerable differences between public and home schools mean that parents will have to assess their own definition of quality education if they are considering either option for their children.

Works Cited

"Benefits of a High School Core Curriculum." Iowa City: American College Testing (ACT) Inc., 2006. PDF.

Bielick, Stacey. *1.5 Million Homeschooled Students in the United States in 2007*. [Washington, D.C.]: U.S. Dept. of Education, Institute of Education Sciences, National Center for Education Statistics, 2008. Print.

Homeschooling Regulations. Digital image. *Times Topics*. The New York Times, 12 Jan. 2008. Web. 6 July 2011. <http://www.nytimes. com/imagepages/2008/01/12/us/20080112_BODIES_GRAPHIC. html>.

"Homeschooling Thru High School." HSLDA – Home School Legal Defense Association, 2011. Web. 05 July 2011. <http://www.hslda. org/highschool/default.asp>.

Ravitch, Diane. "Stop the Madness." *NEA Today Magazine*. National Education Association, Aug. 2010. Web. 23 May 2011. <http://www. nea.org/home/39774.htm>.

Romanowski, Michael H. "Common Arguments about the Strengths and Limitations of Home Schooling." *The Clearing House: A Journal of Educational Strategies*, Issues and Ideas 75.2 (2001): 79–83. Print.

Part 2 | Describing similarities and differences

Words and phrases to describe similarities and differences

In a compare and contrast essay, a variety of words and phrases to describe similarities and differences should be used. Such phrases allow the essay writer to:

- clearly express the similar or contrastive relationship between the subjects being compared.
- reduce repetition of the same words and phrases.

Exercise 1

1. **Brainstorm as many words or phrases as possible for describing similarities and differences.**

    Similarities   Differences

    _____   _____

    _____   _____

    _____   _____

    _____   _____

    _____   _____

    _____   _____

    _____   _____

2. **Read the sample essays on pages 98 and 100. Underline any examples you can find of words or phrases that express a similarity or difference.**

Describing similarities

Words and phrases describing similarities can be grouped according to where they most commonly occur in a sentence.

Phrase	Usage	Example
both X and Y *not only X but also Y*	• To show a similarity between two items • May only occur at the start of the comparative clause or phrase in a sentence • Used in positive sentences	*Both public schools and religious schools teach their pupils about religion through special "religious education" classes.* *Not only religious schools but also public schools teach their pupils about religion through special "religious education" classes.*
neither X nor Y	• To show a similarity between two items • Used in negative sentences	*Neither girls nor boys do particularly well in mathematics in American public schools.*
similarly	• To show a similarity between two items • May be used at the beginning of a sentence (followed by a comma) to indicate similarity with the preceding sentence • May be used in the middle of a sentence before an adjective that applies to both compared items.	*Religious schools place a strong emphasis on teaching moral values. Similarly, teaching religious values is considered a priority.* *Abortion is a controversial issue because some believe it is murder while others believe it is not. The death penalty is a similarly controversial issue because of a debate over whether it is justice or murder.*
also	• To connect two similar ideas • Mostly used in the middle of a sentence in academic essays	*Many parents are worried about the current decline in students' exam results; the government is also beginning to show its concern.*
X is/are similar to Y	• To show a similarity between two nouns • Can be used at the beginning or end of a sentence • Often occurs together with the phrases *in terms of + -ing* or *in that*	*Private schools are similar to public schools in that they have to follow the national curriculum.* *In terms of having to follow the national curriculum, private schools are similar to public schools.*
like	• Used with a noun to show a similarity with a following noun • If used at the beginning of a sentence, the noun after *like* is always followed by a comma	*New Zealand is like Canada in that crime rates are low and standards of living are high.* *Like girls, boys often seem to get higher grades in single-sex schools.*

Exercise 2

Use the words and phrases in the box below to complete the following sentences.

similar to	also	similarly
neither	like	both

1. Parents often have a difficult choice to make because _____ private and public schools have specific advantages and disadvantages.

2. Robinson found that Asian students are _____ North American students in terms of overall academic ability (57).

3. While only 42% of students in Australia were said to be happy with the state of university education, 37% were unhappy with old-fashioned teaching methods such as dictation and use of the blackboard. _____, only 21% of professors believed that their students were "academically strong" (Bell 14).

4. _____ expensive private schools nor free public schools have the resources to provide individual attention to every student who needs it.

5. Boys at same-sex schools showed an increase in motivation and girls _____ benefited from higher levels of concentration.

6. _____ Britain, France has a long-established system of higher education.

Describing differences

Words and phrases describing differences can also be grouped according to where they occur in a sentence.

Phrase	Usage	Example
however *in contrast* *in comparison* *on the other hand*	• To show a contrast between two sentences • Used at the **beginning** of a sentence, followed by a comma, shows the strongest contrast • Used in the **middle** of a sentence, with a comma placed before and after, shows slightly less contrast • Used at the **end** of a sentence, with a comma placed before, shows the least contrast	*Teachers at high school often have a close relationship with their students.* **However,** *professors at university may seem distant or difficult to talk to.* *Teachers at high school often have a close relationship with their students. Professors at university,* **however,** *may seem distant or difficult to talk to.* *Teachers at high school often have a close relationship with their students. Professors at university may seem distant or difficult to talk to,* **however.**
although *though* *whereas* *while*	• Used to show a contrast between two clauses • When used at the beginning of a sentence, a comma must be used to separate the clauses • In the middle of a sentence, a comma may come before *although*	**Although** *public schools provide children with many opportunities to socialize with people from different backgrounds, home schoolers spend more time with their families.* *Public schools provide children with many opportunities to socialize with people from different backgrounds,* **although** *home schoolers spend more time with their families.*
compared to *unlike*	• Used to show a contrast between two nouns • When used at the beginning of a sentence, a comma must be placed at the end of the clause	*Home schooling is more flexible* **compared** *to public school education.* **Compared** *to public school education, home schooling is more flexible.*
but	• Used to show a contrast between two clauses • When used in the middle of a sentence, it should be preceded by a comma • Should not be used at the start of a sentence in academic essays	*University education is provided free for students in Scotland,* **but** *students in England must pay tuition fees.*

Exercise 3

Use the words and phrases in the box below to complete the following sentences.

in contrast	compared to	unlike
however	whereas	but

1. _____ high school, university offers students many opportunities to enjoy their freedom.

2. The education system in Pakistan is divided into five specific levels. _____ , in India the system is divided into three broader levels.

3. High school students in Japan spend around 12% of their school day learning Japanese, _____ American high school students spend only 6% of their time learning English.

4. It is widely believed that private schools offer high-quality education. They cannot guarantee that all students will achieve high scores on their exams, _____ .

5. In Germany, the main responsibility for education lies with individual states within the country. _____ , in France the central government exercises more direct control over education.

6. _____ most public schools, many private schools can offer smaller class sizes and more modern facilities.

Section 2 Parallel structure

When listing, comparing, or contrasting ideas, it is often appropriate to use parallel structure. Using parallel structure means that all items that are listed, compared, or contrasted are expressed **using the same grammatical pattern**. While parallel structure is not always necessary, it is a useful way to ensure that sentences are clear and natural in style. Look at the following examples.

Parallel structure in a list (verbs):

✗ *In single sex schools, boys often have fewer chances to study home economics, practice cheerleading, and <u>they do not take</u> dance classes.*

✓ *In single sex schools, boys often have fewer chances to <u>study</u> home economics, <u>practice</u> cheerleading, or <u>take</u> dance classes.*

Parallel structure of comparative language:

✗ *Alternative schools offer students closer relationships with their teacher, more choice over which subjects to study, and the <u>class sizes are small</u>.*

✓ *Alternative schools offer students <u>closer relationships</u> with their teacher, <u>more choice</u> over which subjects to <u>study</u>, and <u>smaller class sizes</u> than public schools.*

Parallel structure in expressions of comparison

The following phrases are commonly used when comparing two items and should **always use** parallel structure:

- *both X and Y*
- *neither X nor Y*
- *not only X but also Y*

Examples:
Neither <u>taking long breaks</u> **nor** <u>listening to music</u> is possible for students in public school.

Classes in creative subjects such as music are popular **not only** <u>with girls</u> **but also** <u>with boys</u>.

Exercise 4

Read the following sentences. Decide (✓ or ✗) whether each sentence uses parallel structure or not. Correct any sentences that do not use parallel structure.

1. (_____) Some public schools suffer from problems such as bullying, students being absent from school, and sometimes school property is damaged.

2. (_____) Male students may be said to differ from female students both in how they behave in class, and they have lower motivation levels.

3. (_____) Either studying at university or going to a vocational school are options for students who graduate from high school.

4. (_____) Two advantages of home schooling are greater freedom for students to develop their interests, and students have many chances to learn at their own pace.

5. (_____) It is apparent that students in public schools benefit both from contact with students from various backgrounds and the experience of keeping to schedules.

6. (_____) Students not only enjoy many club activities, but also they make many friends.

3 Improving your work

Section 1 — Using commas

As a general rule, the decision about where to place a comma in a sentence depends upon the position of the main subject. If the main subject is not at the beginning of a sentence, it should be preceded by a comma.

Example:

Although they are happy to work in groups, boys often prefer to work individually.

comma   main subject

If the main subject is at the beginning of a sentence, use a comma if it is:

- followed by a non-restrictive clause (see Unit 1, Part 3 page 28) or
- followed by a coordinating conjunction *(for, and, but, or, yet, so)* and another subject and verb.

Example:

main subject ⟶ *Boys, <u>whether in same-sex or coeducational schools,</u> often prefer to work individually.*

non-restrictive relative clause

Boys often prefer to work individually, but <u>they are</u> also happy to work in groups.

main subject   second subject and verb

Circle the main subject in each of the following sentences. Insert commas where appropriate.

1. Unlike girls boys find diagrams easier to understand than wordy explanations.

2. Boys who study in single-sex classes often achieve better results than boys in mixed classes.

3. When listening boys often do not hear as many details as girls.

4. After the lunchtime break both boys and girls often have trouble concentrating in class.

5. While girls often want to be regarded as good students boys are usually less keen to please adults.

6. Girls hear better in class than boys and teachers in all-girl classes are less likely to shout to control their students.

Improving final thoughts

In order to have an impact on the reader, it is important that a final thought serves a clear purpose. A final thought may serve no purpose if:

- it states something which is already simple and obvious to the reader.
- it presents overgeneralizations.
- it is not connected to the thesis of the essay.
- it is not logical.
- it contains subjective language or judgments.
- it attempts to get the reader's agreement.

Example:

> In short, the choice between studying abroad and studying in one's own country can have a strong influence on a student's education intellectually, socially, and economically. Studying in a foreign country can increase a student's independence and expose them to new ways of thinking that they would not encounter at home. Moreover, they can make new friends from different backgrounds – yet they risk growing apart from their friends in their home country. In terms of future career, students who choose to study at home can make many contacts, while students who study abroad may feel pressure to find a job quickly after they return. Therefore, students have to recognize that there are both positive and negative aspects to studying abroad and studying in one's mother country.

In the preceding example, the writer states that both items being compared have "positive and negative aspects." This is an ineffective final thought because:

- it is not specific to the topic of studying abroad because most topics have positive and negative points.
- it does not indicate how positive or negative these aspects are.
- it does not provide the reader with any specific information about the topic.
- there is no real meaning, so this final thought does not have any impact.

To ensure that the final thought serves a clear purpose, it is important to focus on its meaning. The final thought usually highlights the importance or implications of the explanation or argument presented in the essay.

A final thought can be (see Unit 1, Part 2, page 19):

- an opinion.
- a solution.
- a recommendation.
- a prediction.

Exercise 2

Work with a partner. Below are four pairs of final thoughts written for the concluding paragraph on page 110. For each pair, decide whether they are opinions, solutions, recommendations, or predictions. Then decide (✓ or ✗) which final thought in each pair (a or b) is more effective.

1. (_____) *type of final thought*

   a. (_____) Therefore, students who wish to push themselves and become more independent should choose to study abroad while those who enjoy the security of a familiar environment should be happiest studying in their own country.

   b. (_____) Therefore, students who wish to live abroad should choose to study overseas while those who want to keep their childhood friends should stay at home.

2. (_____)

   a. (_____) Although studying abroad can be a rewarding experience, most people would agree that staying in one's own country is by far the best option. It is the best thing for those students who wish to find their dream job.

   b. (_____) Although studying abroad can often be a rewarding experience, there is little doubt that staying in one's own country gives students a more stable education and increases their chances of finding a good job with a domestic company.

3. (_____)

a. (____) As society becomes more globalized, it will become increasingly difficult for students to decide which system is the best.

b. (____) As society becomes more globalized, however, there is little doubt that more and more students will choose to leave their mother country and study abroad as the benefits of this system become increasingly valuable to companies.

4. (_____)

a. (____) Although both systems offer advantages, neither system is perfect. Students are not limited to one choice, however. By choosing to study in one's own country and also to spend one year abroad, students can make the most of their education.

b. (____) Although both systems offer advantages, neither system is perfect. Studying abroad and studying in one's own country both have significant bad points. Students can choose to do both, however, and so they can have a good experience.

Section 2   Revising a compare and contrast essay

The following checklist can be used to edit a compare and contrast essay.

Compare and Contrast Essay Checklist

Whole essay

1. Is the essay an appropriate length?
2. Does the essay follow subject by subject style (5 paragraphs) or point by point style (4 paragraphs)?

Introductory paragraph

3. Is there a hook? Does the hook make the reader want to continue reading?
4. Do the building sentences lead logically to the thesis statement?
5. Does the thesis statement clearly state the reason for comparison and predict the points of comparison?
6. Do the points of comparison logically belong together? Do they help explain the reason for comparison?

Body paragraphs

7. Does the topic sentence show the topic and controlling idea of the paragraph?
8. If subject by subject style is used, does each paragraph focus on one subject only? Are the points of comparison presented in the same order in each paragraph?
9. If point by point style is used, does each paragraph focus on one point of comparison only?
10. Are body paragraphs organized logically using the waltz?
11. Do citations make the author's position stronger?

Concluding paragraph

12. Is the thesis restated?
13. Is there a summary of each main idea from the body paragraphs?
14. Is there a final thought? Does the essay feel completed by this?
15. Are new ideas avoided?

Language/coherence

16. Are words and phrases to describe similarities and differences used appropriately?
17. Are words and phrases to describe similarities and differences punctuated appropriately?
18. Is parallel structure used appropriately?

Using the compare and contrast essay checklist, edit the following sample essay.

Essay question:

Studies have shown that girls consistently outperform boys in school exams, particularly at younger ages. Compare and contrast how boys and girls learn at school to explain this difference.

Boys and girls learn differently. There are many reasons why this may be true. Are boys more open to peer pressure than girls? Are boys generally more energetic, or even more aggressive, than girls? In general, it is true that education is a very important thing for children today. In order to guarantee that each child receives the best possible education, therefore, it is important to consider the different ways in which boys and girls behave in class. Boys and girls can be compared in terms of how they learn, their attitudes in school and they also perform differently.

There is considerable evidence to suggest that boys and girls learn in very different ways. The first significant difference is that boys use fewer words than girls and prefer to work silently on tasks. In contrast, girls enjoy communicating more and are generally more talkative. Perhaps surprisingly, both boys and girls enjoy group work, but their approach to this type of work is different (Baldinger 69). Particularly at younger ages, boys are more physically active than girls and become bored more easily. On the other hand, girls are better at dealing with their boredom without the teacher's attention. Lastly, in comparison to girls, it is clear that boys are more comfortable using abstract concepts.

Another point is that boys and girls have very different attitudes towards school in general. For boys, neither following rules nor respect the teacher is easy. Boys, particularly in their teenage years, are more rebellious than girls. Also, they are more eager to fit in with their peers, rather than to please their teacher. Girls however are more likely to see the teacher as someone they can ask for help. They may even regard their teacher as a friend. Moreover, girls are more self-motivated and tend to take more care with their homework. This is perhaps because they are also more self-critical than boys. But boys seem to view their work as good even when it isn't, and so tend to spend less time trying to make their work "perfect" (Haigh 203).

According to a report by Haigh, "At every level of academic performance, boys are falling behind girls." Everyone knows that boys get worse results than girls in school exams. However, recent evidence suggests that boys' results are stable and have not declined in the last ten years. For instance, Yamada states that, from 1994–2001, boys' results in geography have not shown any considerable change. Of course, boys tend to score high in mathematics and science subjects, so their performances are not as bad as is often suggested. In short, boys' performance does not differ greatly from that of girls.

As we have seen, boys and girls can be compared in terms of how they learn, their attitudes in school, and their academic performance. Firstly, boys are less communicative than girls and also have more problems with boredom. Secondly, boys try less hard to fit in with school rules and girls are more self-motivated. Thirdly and last, although school results are thought to be worse for boys than for girls, this is not always true. In conclusion, both boys and girls have many similarities and differences in their learning styles and so it is very important to consider both.

Worked Cited

"Who does best at school". Kie Yamada. Japan Today. 12 December, 2006.

Haigh, Vicki <u>Learning Differently</u> Donnelly & Hersh. London. 2005.

David Baldinger "Collaborative Learning in Classroom Environments" Wakolbinger Press. Vienna. 2001.

Exercise 4

Read the following first drafts of Essays A and B, comparing and contrasting the performance of boys and girls in high school. Answer the questions for each essay to find the differences between the two.

	Questions	Essay A	Essay B
1	a. Underline the thesis statement. b. Do the topics of the body paragraphs appear in the same order as in the thesis statement?		
2	a. Mark the topic sentences of the body paragraphs with a *TS*. b. Do they clearly indicate what the paragraph will focus on?		
3	a. List the similarities and differences appearing in each paragraph. b. Do they best describe the quality of the two subjects of comparison?		
4	Which pattern has been used, subject by subject or point by point?		
5	a. Mark all the citations with a C. b. Does each citation effectively support a point?		
6	a. Circle all the words and phrases for comparing and contrasting. b. Are they used correctly?		
7	a. Mark all the transitional expressions with a *TE*. b. Are they used correctly?		
8	What needs to be improved in each draft?		

Essay A

Compare and Contrast the Performance of Girls and Boys in High School

Girls tend to get better results in high school and at university because formal education favors girls' natural behaviour, teaching styles in most schools are more suited to girls than boys, and girls tend to be more motivated than boys.

Formal education does not favor boys' natural behavior. Boys are more likely to feel "anti-education" because at school you are expected to be quiet, follow authority, and obey rules. Because boys are encouraged to play sports and be loud outside school, this culture at schools is quite restrictive for boys, so they rebel. On the other hand, girls are expected to talk. Talking and communication are key skills needed at school. Douglas stated that "school is essentially a linguistic experience and most subjects require good levels of comprehension and writing skills" (45). In this way, the current school culture does not seem to be fit for boys.

The second reason for girls' success compared to boys is that the teaching style often favors girls. The majority of high school teachers are female and naturally girls adopt feminine teaching styles better than boys do. Martino and Meyenne said that "gender-conflict is brought to the attention of public schools in various forms" (303). Therefore, teaching styles in most schools contribute to girls' superior academic performance.

It has been pointed out that girls are more motivated and conscientious than boys. They put more effort into their work and spend more time doing homework properly. They take care in how their work is presented.

In conclusion, girls tend to get better academic results at school. Boys should be encouraged to behave like girls.

Essay B

Compare and Contrast the Performance of Girls and Boys in High School

Girls tend to get better results in high school because formal education favors girls' natural behavior, teaching styles in most schools are more suited to girls than boys, and girls tend to be more motivated than boys.

The first reason that girls fare better in school is that the school system tends to favor girls' natural behavior. At school, one is expected to be quiet, accept authority, and follow rules. Whereas girls have this culture imposed on them when they are young, boys do not. Instead, they are often encouraged to play sports, be loud, and be aggressive. On this point, Douglas stated that "girls are raised to be fit for school education while boys are not. Boys are expected to learn how to adopt school culture through the eternal conflicts with school authorities" (199).

Another reason for girls' success compared to boys is that teaching styles often favor girls. Martino and Meyenne (303) said that "boys' performance has been made worse by the feminine influences of female teachers and the very nature of the English curriculum itself." Warrington and Younger also wrote that boys "frequently dominate the classroom environment and do not listen to female teachers" (2000). In this way, feminine teaching styles in most schools contribute to girls' superior academic performance.

A further reason why girls perform better at school than boys is because they are generally more motivated than boys. Mikos and Brown (180) pointed out that girls are more motivated and conscientious than boys. They put more effort into their work and spend more time doing homework properly and they take care in how their work is presented. In contrast, boys do not seem well motivated to submit homework on time (qtd. in Otani 230).

In conclusion, girls achieve better results overall in high school due to the natural tendencies of the school system, the style of feminine teaching in many high schools, and because they are simply better motivated to work hard and learn.

Appendix A

Choosing active or passive sentences

An active sentence has the subject of the sentence doing the action:

1. *Shakespeare wrote* Hamlet *sometime around 1602.*

A passive sentence has the subject of the sentence receiving the action:

2. Hamlet *was written by Shakespeare sometime around 1602.*

In general, active sentences are more direct because they clearly indicate who or what performs an action. However, passive sentences are commonly used in academic writing because they emphasize the "result," "creation," or "discovery" of an action. In the above examples, both sentences are grammatically correct, but the active sentence emphasizes *Shakespeare*, the "doer," while the passive sentence emphasizes *Hamlet*, the creation.

In some cases, especially when the "doer" of the action is **unknown**, or considered **obvious** or **unimportant**, passive sentences are more effective:

3. *Archeologists generally agree that the stones* **were** *purposely* **placed** *in such a way to create a basic calendar.* (doer unknown)
4. *Most of the world's coffee* **is grown** *in Brazil.* (doer obvious)
5. *Even though his experimental results are thought to have* **been manipulated,** *Gregor Mendel* **is** *still* **considered** *the Father of Genetics.* (doer unimportant)

In these cases it is common not to mention the "doer" of the action. Adding the "doer" weakens the main idea of the sentence because the extra information is obvious and is not useful. Compare:

6. *Most of the world's coffee is grown in Brazil.*
7. *Most of the world's coffee is grown in Brazil* **by many farmers.**

In academic writing, use a combination of active and passive sentences to emphasize the information that you consider important.

Practice exercise

Compare sentences a and b. Decide which sentence is more effective.

1.
a. Researchers believe that the manuscript was written in the 10th century.
b. Researchers believe somebody wrote the manuscript in the 10th century.

2.
a. Scientists have discovered that listening to classical music has no effect on children's development.
b. Listening to classical music has been discovered by scientists to have no effect on children's development.

3.
a. Due to globalized supply chains, any given product may be composed of parts produced by workers in factories in many different countries.
b. Due to globalized supply chains, any given product may be composed of parts produced in many different countries.

4.
a. After reporting false information about the government, the journalist was forced to resign.
b. After reporting false information about the government, the owner of the newspaper forced the journalist to resign.

5.
a. Several thousand people were killed in the disaster.
b. The disaster killed several thousand people.

Appendix B

Using conjunctive adverbs

Conjunctive adverbs are transitional words and phrases that are used to show how the meaning of different sentences relate to each other. They can be placed in three different places within a sentence.

Common conjunctive adverbs used in academic writing can be generally grouped by their function:

To express cause and effect		To express contrast between ideas	
accordingly	hence	comparatively	in comparison
as a result	therefore	contrarily	in contrast
consequently	thus	conversely	on the other hand
		however	
To express a continuation of an idea		**To express that one idea does not follow another**	
additionally	furthermore	instead	rather
also	moreover	nevertheless	still
in addition	similarly	nonetheless	
further	thereafter		
To express emphasis		**To express sequence**	
equally	notably	finally	
in particular	particularly	henceforth	
indeed	specifically	subsequently	
namely	undoubtedly		

The position of conjunctive adverbs in a sentence can make meaning clearer by emphasizing or de-emphasizing words. Compare the following examples:

1. *People in Brazil speak Portuguese.* **However,** *people in the rest of South America mainly speak Spanish.*
2. *People in Brazil speak Portuguese. People in the rest of South America,* **however,** *mainly speak Spanish.*
3. *People in Brazil speak Portuguese. People in the rest of South America mainly speak Spanish,* **however**.

Example 1 emphasizes the contrast between the information in the two sentences.
Example 2 emphasizes that the subject is different – that "People in the rest of South America" are different from people in Brazil.
Example 3 reduces the strength of the contrast.

Practice exercises

1. **In each of the five examples, find three places in the second sentence where conjunctive adverbs (in parenthesis) can be added:**

   a. (However) Many people associate bananas with South America. India is actually the country that produces the most bananas.

   b. (Therefore) Most bananas grown in India are consumed domestically. India is not well known as an exporter of bananas.

   c. (As a result) Bananas are a good source of energy, vitamin B6, and potassium. Many athletes eat them as part of a nutritionally balanced diet.

   d. (In fact) The bananas that you see in the supermarket are usually yellow with brown spots which show that they are ready to be eaten. Thanks to technology, bananas can be harvested up to one month earlier and are transported in special refrigerated containers to prevent ripening.

   e. (On the other hand) In Europe and North America, ripe bananas are eaten as fruit or used in deserts. In many tropical countries, bananas are eaten green and cooked like potatoes.

2. **Add appropriate conjunctive adverbs to the following passage. Consider where they can be placed in the sentence for emphasis.**

   Many South American countries are banana exporters. The most common variety of banana found in supermarkets today is the Dwarf Cavendish. Until the 1950s, another variety, Gros Michel, was the most popular around the world. It was almost completely wiped out by a leaf disease. The Cavendish banana is resilient against the disease, and became the most commonly grown. Cavendish bananas are all genetically identical. Scientists think there is a realistic possibility that they too could be susceptible to disease and be wiped out in the future. Efforts are being undertaken in Honduras to develop new, disease resilient varieties of banana.

Appendix C

Using acronyms and initialisms

Acronyms and initialisms are abbreviations which are normally based on the first letter or letters of each word. They are often abbreviations for the names of organizations, companies, and medical conditions.

Acronyms are pronounced as a word. For example:

AIDS – **a**cquired **i**mmune **d**eficiency **s**yndrome
NATO – **N**orth **A**tlantic **T**reaty **O**rganization

NOTE: some acronyms have become regular words:

scuba – **s**elf-**c**ontained **u**nderwater **b**reathing **a**pparatus
radar – **ra**dio **d**etection **a**nd **r**anging

Initialisms are pronounced by each letter. For example:

TGV – **T**rain à **G**rande **V**itesse (French high-speed train)
ALS – **a**myotrophic **l**ateral **s**clerosis

When using an acronym or initialism for the first time, spell it out in full and then write the abbreviation in parenthesis directly after it. After that, use the abbreviation. If the complete term is only used once in the essay, do not write the acronym because you will not be referring to it again; simply write the term out in full:

*Medecins Sans Frontieres (MSF) was founded in France in 1971. It provides medical assistance in areas affected by war or natural disaster. It is a non-governmental organization and receives the majority of its funding from private donations. In 1999, **MSF** was awarded the Nobel Prize for Peace in recognition of its humanitarian work.*

In this example, the initialism for Medecins Sans Frontieres is given because it is referred to again. The initialism for a non-governmental organization (NGO) is not given, as it is only used once.

Practice exercise

Correct the mistakes with the use of acronyms and initialisms in the following paragraph.

After World War II, Spain has played a role in numerous influential international organizations in economic, military, and sporting areas. It became part of the United Nations, UN, in 1955, when member countries saw it as a valuable ally in the Cold War. Spain now contributes to international UN aid efforts, such as making grants to developing countries in order to encourage climate change measures, and is one of the top five United Nations contributors in aid for human rights. After becoming a democracy, Spain joined the North Atlantic Treaty Organization in 1982, and was seen as a valuable ally due to its important strategic position next to the Mediterranean Sea and the Strait of Gibraltar. Spanish forces contributed to NATO operations in both Iraq and Afghanistan. Finally, there is the contribution to the International Olympics Committee (IOC). The second longest serving president of this organization was a Spaniard named Juan Antonio Samaranch, who served from 1980 to 2001.

Appendix D

Placing adverbs of frequency

There are many adverbs that express how often something happens. Below is a list of the most common:

always	occasionally	usually
rarely	frequently	seldom
often	hardly ever	sometimes
never		

The position of adverbs of frequency generally follows these rules:

Before a single verb:

1. *Unlike symptoms of a common cold, flu symptoms <u>usually begin</u> suddenly.*

After the verb to be:

2. *Dolphins are highly intelligent mammals and <u>are often</u> friendly to divers.*

After an auxiliary verb:

3. *Revolutions <u>have rarely</u> been achieved without bloodshed.*
4. *Hereditary diseases <u>can often</u> skip a generation.*

At the beginning of sentences (not all adverbs):

5. *<u>Occasionally</u>, some elephants will eat coconuts and sugar cane.*

Note that the position of adverbs of frequency affects what is emphasized in a sentence. Compare the following examples:

6. *Some elephants will <u>occasionally</u> eat coconuts and sugar cane.*
7. *<u>Occasionally</u>, some elephants will eat coconuts and sugar cane.*

An adverb placed at the beginning of the sentence can emphasize the frequency of the action over the subject performing the action.

Also note that when a negative adverb is used at the start of a sentence, it causes a subject-verb inversion. Compare the following examples:

8. *African elephants rarely look for food in the same area for more than a few days.*
9. *<u>Rarely</u> do African elephants look for food in the same area for more than a few days.*
10. *Attempts to breed elephants in zoos are seldom successful.*
11. *<u>Seldom</u> are attempts to breed elephants in zoos successful.*

Practice exercises

1. **From the adverbs listed on the previous page, make three categories:**

   a. Adverbs which cannot start a sentence.

   b. Adverbs which do not require a comma after them when they start a sentence.

   c. Adverbs which require a comma after them when they begin a sentence.

2. **Look at the following sentences. If the sentence is correct, write ✓. If the sentence is incorrect, write ✗ and then decide how to correct the mistake.**

   a. _____ Although bears in the wild will sometimes approach humans, they try to avoid people usually.

   b. _____ Though initially banned by many schools, *The Catcher in the Rye* is frequently read in American high school English classes today.

   c. _____ Never, are people legally permitted to operate an automobile without first obtaining a driver's license.

   d. _____ Grits, a common breakfast delicacy in the southeastern United States, are hardly found in restaurants in northern states ever.

   e. _____ Failing to pay attention to the road often is a factor in traffic accidents.

3. **Place the adverb in parenthesis in an appropriate place in the following sentences:**

   a. (seldom) Although there are exceptions, professional athletes go through their entire career without sustaining an injury.

   b. (always) The most diverse ecosystems have been found in tropical rain forests.

   c. (occasionally) Taking short breaks during the workday has been shown by some studies to boost productivity.

   d. (often) Able to elude researchers, the giant squid is an animal still shrouded in mystery.

Appendix E

Using quantifiers

Quantifiers express the number or amount of the noun they precede. It is common to use quantifiers when the exact number is unimportant or unknown.

Quantifiers used with **countable nouns**:

many (of the)	*Many of the animals* were captured in the wild.
a few (of the)	*A few of the animals* have room to roam.
few (of the)	*Few of the large animals* have enough space.
several (of the)	*Several of the animals* have contracted diseases.
a couple of (the)	*A couple of animals* have become ill due to poor diets.
none of the	*None of the animals* <u>appear</u> to be happy in the zoo. *(singular verb)*
each (of the)	*Each bear* has distinct personality traits.
every (of the)	*Every bear* trying to escape has been caught.
a number of (the)	*A number of visitors* have viewed the monkeys recently.
the number of	*The number of visitors* to zoos <u>has</u> decreased. *(singular verb)*

Quantifiers used with uncountable nouns:

a little	*A little* more **effort** will be required before any progress is made.
little	*Little progress* has been made due to lack of effort.
a good deal of	They acquired **a good deal of expertise** working with the Welsh miners.
a great deal of	*A great deal of effort* was required to separate the angry hippos.
much (only negative)	The NGO did **not** have **much time** to react to the new law.
much of the	*Much of the staff* became ill after eating the tainted meat.

Quantifiers used with countable and uncountable nouns:

all (of the)	*All of the snacks* <u>were</u> / **food** <u>was</u> eaten by a band of monkeys.
some (of the)	*Some of the chairs* <u>were</u> / **furniture** <u>was</u> imported from Italy.
most (of the)	*Most diamond rings* <u>are</u> / **jewelry** <u>is</u> actually quite affordable.
a lot of	The group was given **a lot of chances** / **time** to reform its policies.

Gradable Quantifiers:

Used with plural countable nouns:	many, more, most
Used with uncountable nouns:	much, more, most
Used with plural countable nouns:	few, fewer, fewest
Used with uncountable nouns:	little, less, least

Practice exercises

1. **Find and correct any mistakes in the following sentences. Some sentences may not have any mistakes.**

   a. Much of the people attending the conference had traveled from countries outside the United States.

   b. A great deal of animals have been endangered due to human development and migration.

   c. Almost all of the students who were asked were unwilling to take part in the experiment, but few of them agreed to participate.

   d. Underfunded schools are at a disadvantage because little of their textbooks are the most current.

   e. Even though they signed the free trade agreement, each country still have some taxes on imports.

   f. The company secured several important contracts last year, so they gave large bonuses to some of employees.

2. **Fill in the blanks with an appropriate quantifier.**

   a. According to the study, although _____ of the members taking the drug reported a reduction in symptoms, _____ of those taking the placebo also reported feeling better. Therefore, _____ research is needed before the drug's effect can be fully understood. However, because _____ money and time are required, and because there is _____ public funding for experimental psychiatric medicines, further experiments are not planned for the near future.

   b. After viewing the film, 60 percent of audiences said that they thought the film had too _____ violence. However, despite the fact that they thought it had _____ content which might be inappropriate for minors, _____ viewers said they would consider allowing their children to see the film due to its overall moral message.

   c. Although _____ people say they wish to climb Mt. Everest at some point in their lives, relatively _____ people actually achieve their goal. One reason _____ those who wish to go decide not to is because of the _____ dangers involved.

Appendix F

Using punctuation

The period or full stop (.)
Used to indicate the end of a complete sentence:

1.   *The maple leaf is a symbol of Canada.*

The comma (,)
Used when listing a series of three or more words or phrases:

2.   *The founding members of the European Economic Community were Belgium, the Federal Republic of Germany, France, Italy, Luxembourg, and the Netherlands.*
3.   *Native languages spoken in Latin America include Quechua, Guarani, Garifuna, and Yucatec.*

NOTE: The **serial comma** is placed before the last item in a list to ensure the item is not connected to the others. Compare the following examples:

4.   *Society's elite prohibited men without property and women from voting or having any kind of political involvement.*
5.   *Society's elite prohibited men without property, and women from voting or having any kind of political involvement.*

serial comma

In example 4, the meaning of the sentence implies men had to own property and own women. Example 5 makes it clear that there were two separate groups who could not vote or have any political involvement: men without property in one group, and women in the other.

Used to form compound sentences by connecting two independent clauses with a coordinating conjunction:

6.   *The political climate was not right for an election, so the prime minister waited for another year.*

NOTE: Two independent clauses cannot be connected with only a comma.

7.   ✗   *The political climate was not right for an election, the prime minister waited for another year.*
They can, however, be connected with a semicolon, as in example 12.

Used with subordinating conjunctions to form complex sentences by connecting a dependent clause to an independent clause when the dependent clause comes first:

8.   ***Whereas*** *Spanish is the most studied foreign language in U.S. schools, students in the U.K. most commonly study French as a foreign language.*

If the independent clause comes first, the comma is not needed:

9. *Spanish is the most studied foreign language in U.S. schools **whereas** students in the U.K. most commonly study French as a foreign language.*

Used to form non-restrictive relative clauses. These are clauses which give additional, but not essential, information about a noun:

10. *The tiger, which is found throughout the Indian Subcontinent, is a fearsome and formidable predator.*

Compare example 10 to the following example of a restrictive relative clause. In this case a specific tiger is being referred to and therefore commas are not used:

11. *The tiger which killed the goats yesterday is also thought to have attacked several other herds in recent weeks.*

The semicolon (;)

Used to form compound sentences by joining two independent clauses. This is an alternative method instead of using a co-ordinating or subordinating conjunction, or a transitional adverb:

12. *The political climate was not right for an election; the prime minister waited for another year.*

The colon (:)

Used to connect words or phrases to a complete sentence, such as a list of examples, short explanatory sentences, or long quotations:

13. *In the annual future career survey of junior high school students, the most popular choices were unchanged from last year: doctor, computer game developer, comic artist, and entertainer.*
14. *Environmentalism means more than just being concerned about the world: it is a way of life.*

NOTE: It is also common for a **hyphen (–)** to be used in place of a colon:

15. *Environmentalism means more than just being concerned about the world – it is a way of life.*

The apostrophe (')

Used to form possessives. Before the -s with most nouns:

16. *Shakespeare's first play*

After the -s with plural nouns:

17. *The students' work*

For proper nouns that end in an -s, after the -s **or** before an additional -s:

18. *Columbus' voyage **or** Columbus's voyage*
19. *Xenophanes' philosophy **or** Xenophanes's philosophy*

Capitalization (uppercase)

Used for:

a. The first word of a sentence: *It was a momentous day.*

b. The pronoun "I": *He does, but I do not.*

c. Proper nouns: *South Africa, Tokyo Tower, Thomas Hardy*

d. Official titles: *President Wilson, King Sejong, Admiral Nelson*

e. First and significant words of a title: *The Three Sisters, The Siege of Krishnapur, Once Upon a Time in America*

f. Holidays and festivals: *Ramadan, Easter, Purim, Boxing Day*

g. Key religious terms: *Buddhism, the Qur'an, the Tanakh*

h. Brand names and companies: *Porsche, Coca-Cola*

i. Historical periods: *the Middle Ages, the Edo period, the Ming dynasty*

j. Names of languages: *Farsi, Swahili, Korean, Turkish*

k. Days and months: *Monday, September*

l. Roman numerals (except when listing information in bullet points): XXVII

m. National or ethnic groups: *Indonesians, the Inuit, French bread*

Practice exercise

In the following paragraph, add periods, commas, semi-colons, colons, apostrophes, and capital letters where necessary.

while rising sea levels will cause major problems for developed countries in the long term it is developing countries with large areas of low-lying coastal land such as bangladesh vietnam and egypt which face the more immediate threat firstly the increased sea levels will lead to a reduction in the space which is available for living for example it has been noted that 27% of bangladeshs habitable land will be lost by 2100 as a result of the rise in sea levels this will lead to a much higher level of population density secondly as a result of the rising sea levels large areas of the countries agricultural land which is often located in the coastal regions will become unusable for instance leatherman estimates that 16% of egypts agricultural land could be lost by 2100 consequently these countries will find it difficult to provide enough food to support their populations it is clear that rapid action needs to be taken in order to protect these developing countries from the devastating effects of rising sea levels

Appendix G

Using negating prefixes

Many verbs and adjectives can express their negative meaning by adding an appropriate prefix. Instead of writing "not...," a prefix such as **un-, non-, im-, in-, ir-, il-, dis-,** and **mis-** creates a more concise and formal word that carries the same negative meaning.

1. ✗ *They were **not able** to reach a compromise.*
   ✓ *They were **unable** to reach a compromise.*

2. ✗ *The substance was later found to be **not poisonous**.*
   ✓ *The substance was later found to be **nonpoisonous**.*

3. ✗ *The company was **not honest** about how much oil leaked into the ocean.*
   ✓ *The company was **dishonest** about how much oil leaked into the ocean.*

4. ✗ *It was decided to **not continue** negotiations.*
   ✓ *It was decided to **discontinue** negotiations.*

5. ✗ *The likelihood of such an event occurring is **not probable**.*
   ✓ *The likelihood of such an event occurring is **improbable**.*

6. ✗ *After the public outcry, the researchers claimed that their findings were **not interpreted** properly.*
   ✓ *After the public outcry, the researchers claimed that their findings were **misinterpreted**.*

In your writing, check for instances when "not ..." is used, and consider the possibility of removing it and adding a prefix. However, check to be sure the new word expresses exactly what you want to say because adding a prefix can sometimes change the meaning of the word and the sentence.

Practice exercise

Read the following sentences. If you can replace the "not" with a prefix without changing the meaning of the sentence, do so. If the "not" cannot be replaced without changing the meaning of the sentence, do not make any changes.

1. Although sharks have a bad reputation, 329 of the 354 different species of shark are not dangerous to humans.

2. One necessary step along the path to economic development is reducing the number of people who are not literate.

3. Although fun to drive, sports cars are notorious for not being reliable.

4. Proper journalists must avoid using sources which are not credible.

5. Because they have the option of spending their free time using increasingly sophisticated video game technology, many children are not interested in playing outside on the weekends.

6. The scientists felt that their results were not represented correctly by the media.

7. Because of its difficulty, particle physics is not understood by many people.

8. Much of the human genome is not different from that of other living organisms.